# *THE*
# *RENEGADE*

## FROM THE GUTTERMOST TO THE UTTERMOST

## Floyd Ridley

### WITH ABIGAIL CONDON

# THE RENEGADE

From the Guttermost to the Uttermost

ISBN 978-168454158-4

*This book is dedicated to Pastors Nathan and Joie Miller for showing me that I had gifts that I was not aware of—and how to use those gifts in my ministry to make it more powerful. They both have been great mentors to me and my ministry, and I will be forever grateful to them.*

Doug & Barb,

God Bless

Floyd Bradley

# Contents

# *Foreword by*

## CANONSBURG POLICE CHIEF
## ALEXANDER COGHILL

AS A POLICE OFFICER, I fell into the usual trap of thinking—where skepticism, suspicion, and cynicism dominate your every thought about your fellow man.

You quickly learn that pedophiles gravitate to playgrounds and the Internet, drug dealers are on the corners, some families should never get together, and drunks are found in bars.

I began my career as a police officer nearly 30 years ago as a patrolman. Like most officers, I worked all the shifts and got to know all the trouble areas and trouble people. This is when I met Floyd.

Back then the whole department knew him as "Sarge," and on any given morning, he could be found dangerously staggering in and out of traffic trying to make it home. It was so bad that the officers usually brought him home because they didn't want to find him dead in the middle of the road. If I were a betting man, I would have wagered back then that someday soon the call would come.

A few years passed, and we heard nothing more from Floyd. I often wondered what had become of him. By this time, I was a detective, no longer patrolling the streets, and had Floyd figured for dead.

Then, one day, as I was having coffee at a local diner, he came walking in, with no stagger. He came over to me and started telling me about how he had changed his life and was now sober. He told me he had gotten his driver's license and had reconciled with his family; and, most importantly, found his Savior, Jesus Christ. At first, I felt proud of him, but soon after, that old "cop" cynicism set in, and I laughed it off, figuring he would be like the rest. If I had a nickel for every drunk or drug addict who told me they were "clean," I would have retired years ago.

Fast forward 15 years. I am now the chief of police. Floyd is still sober and a person I call a friend. More than that, he has become an expert in recovery and lives to help others in crisis. He has been that one beacon of light who single-handedly changed my cynical attitude.

He is a true community leader who gives selflessly to those in crisis.

**ALEXANDER COGHILL**

*Floyd, age 3, (bottom left) and some of his siblings pose outside their home in Milford, PA.*

# 1

## SPRING 1958

THE JOURNEY BEGAN November 3, 1944, the day I was born.

They say where you grow up defines who you are and where you end up. Good home, loving family equals a college degree, job, and happy marriage. Bad home, dysfunctional family, equals—well, the opposite.

Our house—I won't call it a home—was a church. Well, it once was a church, before somebody decided to pick it up and move it from the banks of the Delaware River. I guess the old church kept on flooding. By the time they moved it up to Milford, it was too damaged to be used as a church anymore. It was a fitting beginning—being flooded may have been the best memory that house ever had.

Once they abandoned the church for a newer one down the road, the congregation tried to fix it up and turn it into a two-family townhouse, each unit separated by some thin walls and peeling wallpaper.

I sure hope that those church people did a better job taking care of their new building than they did of our house. Even if my parents had bothered to clean the whole thing top to bottom, it still would have looked dirty. As a child, I figured that if I were God, I'd be glad that this dump was no longer called a church. I bet that He was glad to get rid of it. I woke up in that house almost every morning for the first sixteen years of my life. Some of the good days started in that house, but so did a bunch of the worst. But there is one day that, for the longest time, I couldn't quite place in a category. Was it a good day? Was it a bad day?

I guess it all depends on your perspective and whether you look at that day as just one day, or you see it as the beginning of the rest of my life.

I was thirteen. On that day, I wiped the sleep from my eyes, tried to get out of bed without waking up my younger brothers—who shared the twin bed with me—and walked down the stairs to the kitchen. I tried my best not to make any noise. Not because of my brothers. They probably wouldn't have cared much, but because my mother was probably still sleeping, hungover in the master bedroom.

Outside, I saw my father hanging some wash on the line, just like he did every Sunday. The faded shirts and hole-ridden jeans hung limp on the line, laden with water. I rolled my eyes and silently hoped that no could see him doing what should have been my mother's work.

There were many things my mother should have been doing, things the mothers on TV always did, things my friends' mothers did. Like cleaning and cooking, taking us to church and teaching us to keep our elbows off the table. But this day, she wouldn't be doing any of those things. There would be no church. There would be no hugs or freshly-baked cookies as we returned from playing outside.

I opened the cabinet and pulled out a box of cereal. As I did, something scurried from behind the box and disappeared into the corner of the cupboard. It could have been a roach or a mouse, though the hole in the bottom corner of the box seemed too small for a mouse. I poured myself a bowl of cereal and added some milk, checking briefly to make sure that there weren't any visible animal droppings, then checking again to make sure I had left enough for my younger brothers to get a serving.

As I ate, I heard my father come in, head upstairs, and turn on the water in the bathroom. When I was younger, I had visions of my father tousling my hair, asking me how I slept, and maybe inviting me to play ball with him after he finished fixing the car, but by now, I knew that he just wasn't that kind of man.

I ate quickly, anticipating what my day might hold if I just left before my father finished showering and my mother woke up. I slurped the leftover milk from the bottom of the bowl and ignored my still-growling stomach as I tried to find some clothes that seemed clean. I threw on my fake leather coat, put my stolen cigarettes in my pocket, and left the house. I wasn't exactly sure where I was going, but I was very sure I wasn't going to sit inside all day waiting for my parents to start drinking.

During the day, my siblings and I would do anything to get out of the house. We would head down to the ballfield and try to join a game. We would stop by our friends' houses, scrounge around to find enough money for a movie…anything that didn't require us to wait at home.

To get into town, I had to walk past the Methodist church—the church that had replaced my house a few decades before.

As I walked down the street, I saw a mother dressed in a long, flowing dress ushering along two toddlers as a father led the family into the building. The music was already started and, while the father looked a bit rushed, the mother smiled and softly coaxed her children to "walk quickly now, darlings" and "be sure to be quiet once we get inside!"

As I passed by, I heard the soft sound of the door closing, putting the nice family and all their fellow church-goers inside, and leaving me alone on the sidewalk. I could hear people singing along with the organ.

According to the missionary lady who led Sunday school classes in the park by the church, songs people sang in church were called hymns. She had tried to teach them to us, but I only went to her services because she gave away free cookies. I had already decided that if there was a God, he didn't like me.

I walked to the baseball field first to see if anyone I knew was playing. When I arrived, it looked like a few families had decided to play a baseball game together. The moms sat at picnic tables, smiling and cheering on their sons. When they noticed me, I saw a few of their smiles falter. One boy I knew started to wave at me, but his mother quickly pulled his hand down. I didn't have to be close to know what she was saying. I had heard it all before. "He's bad news. I don't want you playing with that Ridley boy."

That's the reputation you got when your parents spent more time at the bar than anywhere else.

I kept walking, wondering what it would have been like for my parents to take me and my siblings out to the park like this.

My parents almost never took us to the park and it was, frankly, okay. One day, I had been down at the ballfield playing with my friends when suddenly we all saw a small, stumbling woman running toward us, cursing and yelling.

I prayed. *Please God, if You're real, don't let that be my mom. Please, don't let it be Mom.*

I heard my friends snickering behind me. "Oh no, here comes Floyd's mother!"

"Gosh, not again!"

"You little son of a—" she yelled. "Get home right now!" I rolled my eyes, wondering why she needed me home. There was nothing to do there, and she certainly wouldn't be spending time with me.

I looked toward my friends apologetically. Some of them looked annoyed; others looked like they just felt bad for me. I hated that feeling. I hated being pitied. If my mother hadn't been right there, I probably would have beaten-up, at least, one of them for looking at me like that. If there was one thing I knew, it was that no one would laugh at Floyd Ridley.

People laughing at me or my family had always been a pet peeve of mine. Of course, I knew most of the neighborhood laughed at us. Most people had seen my parents down at the bar making fools of themselves every night of the week. For some reason, that seemed to make people think that they could get away with saying bad things about my parents in front of me or mocking the way my siblings and I had to live our lives.

People just didn't know how to keep their mouths shut and mind their own business.

When I was young, they would take any chance they got to try to take a cheap jab at me. I remember being at lunch and watching all the other kids go get lunch from the cafeteria workers, and the ones who didn't buy lunch would bring out packed lunches with sandwiches and fruit kept inside shiny lunch tins.

I ate the same thing every day—a butter sandwich. I always

tried to pull it out and eat it quickly, before anyone could notice or make a snide remark. I would keep it in my coat and pull it out just far enough so that I could get a quick bite. That was all we usually had in the house, and my parents definitely didn't spend money for me to have food at the school.

Then I heard a voice, loud enough so I could hear it.

"Hey, Floyd, what do you have there? What is that, butter?" Everyone laughed.

"Look at Floyd over there eating a butter sandwich for lunch!" I tried to ignore him.

"What's the matter? Can't even afford peanut butter?"

My blood boiled, and before he could react, I punched him. Hard. *Bam!*

He fell down.

Eyes widened around me. Whispers hit my ears from every direction. "Did you see him?"

"He hit him straight into next week!"

"Somebody get Miss Brown!"

"No way! He'll hit you next if you do!"

Stephen put a hand to his face. Checking for blood, I assumed. Finding none, he stood up again and looked at me. His shoulders hunched slightly, but his eyes were fierce.

My hand was still frozen in a fist. No way was I backing down. I took a step toward him. Stephen took three quick steps backward, almost falling into the lunch table that he had been sitting at.

I kept my eyes on him. "Next time, I break your nose," I said. Then I turned around and walked back to my seat.

That wasn't the last time someone made fun of me. Of course, I couldn't really blame them because my family gave them plenty of opportunities.

Sometimes, my dad forgot to do the wash, or he'd get halfway through before he started drinking. Sometimes, he'd forget about it and our clothes would mildew. Every time we moved, they released a plant-like smell.

Again, in a voice just loud enough so that I could hear, they said, "Floyd, you stink! You've got to wash those clothes!" Everyone around me would giggle and snicker and then Bam! I'd hit another one of them. I'd keep the fight short and clean, so the teachers wouldn't get involved. But the other kids had to know that they weren't going to mess with me.

By this point, some of the kids who'd made fun of me showed some respect. They now rushed past me in the hall, heads down so I wouldn't see them. Even the teachers seemed a little bit afraid. I knew that I didn't want to really hurt anyone, and I was too skinny to do much damage anyway. I didn't fight about fear, though. I fought for respect. I wanted people to know that they didn't get to treat me differently than they treated anyone else.

Maybe that's why it was so frustrating to see all those moms look at me like I was the devil himself. What did they think, that I was going to grab their toddler by the hand and throw him on the ground? Did they think that I was going to teach them how to steal cigarettes and beer from their parents? Did I really look so bad that they couldn't even offer me a polite wave? Or even just a smile?

I walked a little faster, down the main drag, when I saw a man sitting on the side of the road. I knew that he was a drunk too. It always amazed me that there could be such a difference between the people on the street and my parents. Who decided that my parents would somehow have enough money to live in an apartment with their five youngest kids and that this man would sit on the side of the road all day looking for money?

I had seen this man around before. We knew him as the town wino. I had walked by him before, but today I stopped. He didn't look at me. He just stared at the brown paper bag in his hands. "Move on, buddy. This ain't a circus." He still didn't look at me.

I shuffled my feet and the wino looked up. "What's your deal, kid?"

"How much to get a bottle of wine?" I asked him, startled that the words I had been thinking in my head had traveled out my mouth. "You think you could get one?"

"For you?" he asked.

"Yeah, who's askin'?"

He looked around for a moment then answer, "Give me enough for two bottles. One for me, one for you." I didn't know exactly how much that would be, so I hesitated. My hesitation seemed to annoy him. "I'm not gettin' it for free," he said.

Startled, I rummaged through my pockets and pulled out everything I had and handed it over.

"Wait here," he said, pushing himself up, still holding on to his brown paper bag.

While I waited, I imagined what it was going to taste like. I had drunk beer before, and I liked it. My father always kept some in a cooler inside our house.

A few months before, I had taken out a bottle when no one was looking and drunk it all. It was cool and refreshing, and I wanted to drink more of it. I didn't feel very much different. Didn't feel happier, didn't feel angrier. Felt just like regular old Floyd.

And even though it hadn't done anything to me, I knew it had the power to make things feel different than the way they were. She never told me so, but I knew that was the reason my mother drank. Maybe it was because her parents and siblings had already died, or maybe her childhood was bad too. Whatever it was, I knew enough to know that she didn't have to think about any of that when she was drunk.

After what seemed like a long time, the man finally returned, handing me my bottle of wine. I held the bottle in my hands, thanked him, and quickly continued down the road. I headed to the school, which was built so that there weren't a lot of houses or anything near the back side of it. I sat down with my bottle and my cigarettes. I lit a cigarette first, taking a long drag, letting the smoke relax me, then I opened the bottle. It was sweet. Much sweeter than beer, but just as delicious, and even more refreshing.

For the next hour or so I sat there. Sipping and smoking. Thinking about my life, and my parents. Thinking about the times when they had failed in every possible way. Wishing I could get away, like I did every day.

And then I realized it had been twenty minutes and I hadn't thought about my parents or my house, or my teachers, or anybody who had done me wrong. When I realized that I was so far away from my problems, I felt like I was floating. First there was peace, and then I started laughing. Everything was fine and everything was funny. What parents? What rats? What emptiness? I sat there laughing by myself for hours. I laughed until I threw up, and then I laughed again because the whole situation was funny. When the world stopped spinning, I went home.

The feeling was indescribable. Imagine the most intense longing that you have ever had. Like wanting a certain present for Christmas as a child or waiting to marry the love of your life. When that desire is fulfilled, your brain can hardly focus. You're euphoric. Even if something bad happened, you would barely know it, because you are safe; you have everything you've ever wanted. Nothing can hurt you. Finally, no matter what's waiting for you when you get home, no matter whether or not you get to eat a real meal, no matter what, you're going to be all right.

And that's what every child wants. In fact, it's probably the only thing children want. It's just that most kids are treated well by their parents, so they never even think about what it would be like to not know everything was going to be okay.

I knew it was all I had wanted for the last thirteen years, and that day, in a 24 ounce bottle of wine, I found it.

Why? With wine, nothing mattered. My parents didn't matter. My teachers didn't matter. My reputation didn't matter. My failures didn't matter.

If I had been a different kid, I might have wondered if I was the reason my parents were alcoholics. Lucky for me, I knew they'd picked up that bad habit long before I came around, though I did seem to bring out the worst in them. No matter what I did, my mother never seemed to be happy with me. Maybe it was me, maybe it was because she was drunk. Why worry about the reason? I remember my mother being drunk when dropping me off for the first day of kindergarten. We must have been fighting about something, though I probably couldn't have told you what it was, because she dragged me into the class by the ear.

"Here," she spat. "You take care of this little renegade."

Nowadays, that might raise some eyebrows, but nobody paid much attention to the spectacle. They just showed me to my seat and told my mother they would take good care of me.

As I sat at my small desk in a square with the other kids, coloring a picture with sharp new crayons, I noticed the teacher standing over me. I looked up at her, and she knelt down, holding eye contact with me. Her smile radiated into her bright, kind eyes.

"Well look here, we have another Arty. I bet you really look up to your big brother, huh?"

I nodded, not sure what to make of her sudden interest in me or my brother. But she was smiling! It had been a long time since a woman had looked at me with such a nice smile. Even my sisters didn't smile much.

"I had your brother in my class a couple of years ago." She gently tapped the desk with her right index finger and said, "He sat right in this desk. My goodness...you look just like him."

I had heard that all of us Ridley boys looked alike before, so I just nodded. "Well, if you're anything like your brother, I think we're going to have a great year." She gave me one last smile and then stood up. "All right, class, let's come on up to the carpet for a story to start our first day!"

I didn't want to tell that sweet teacher right away, but she would soon find out that I was *not* just like my brother Arty. In fact, we were probably the two most different boys in the entire Ridley family. He was obedient and athletic. I was rail thin and downright rebellious. But I didn't want her to know that. In fact, I wanted her to think I was Arthur 2.0 for as long as I could.

I plastered a smile on my face and bounced to the carpet, following every direction as well as I could. And I was the best Arthur I could be...for the first few weeks. I was happy, the teachers were happy, and even my parents seemed a little happier.

But then, we started the lessons and the teachers got more and more strict with their rules. Letters were easy enough, but it seemed as if everybody had already learned what we were learning, and I was already two steps behind.

I couldn't keep up, and after a few weeks of struggling, I just decided I didn't want to keep up. Every time I asked a question, I could see in my teacher's eyes that I was not the boy she was hoping I was. I wasn't even the boy *I* was hoping I was. And I'm sorry to say that the rest of elementary school was worse than that first year.

After a while, my mother got so sick of hearing about all the bad things I was doing that she decided to send me to church.

I probably told you that my family wasn't at all religious. That's not entirely true. My mother was a Catholic in word only. The only time that I spent inside a church was when she would drag me to the doors of the convent and throw me at the nuns. For all that alcohol seemed to fix in her life, she felt that church was the only choice for me.

The nuns signed me up for catechism after school every day. And I figured, if I had to be there, I may as well have some fun. The priest started talking about Jesus and how he was born of a virgin.

"How come none of the girls use that excuse nowadays?" I whispered to the boy next to me, who almost burst out laughing, but managed to cover his mouth in time to stifle the noise.

The priest's eyes darted toward us, a silent warning.

"Floyd, don't get us in trouble," the boy whispered, still holding back a laugh.

I whispered back, "What could the penguins do to us that our parents haven't already done?"

"Mr. Ridley, come here," said the priest. I had always thought priests were supposed to be quiet, holy people. But the tone of his voice sounded anything but quiet and holy. I strode toward him, confident, ready to take whatever punishment he could possibly dole out. That was one thing I had learned at school. Getting in trouble won't ruin your reputation, but the way you handle yourself while you're getting punished will.

In school, we had a rule where if you got in trouble with the teacher, you either had to kiss her on the cheek or take five whacks on your hands. All the boys who were afraid of pain kissed the teacher. They would flush red with embarrassment and dart their eyes down. Weak.

When I would get in trouble, I would stroll to the front of the class like they were about to give me an award. I held out my hands and took the whacks with a smile on my face. My hands were burning, no doubt about that, but I knew that nothing could hurt me. No word, no punch, no nothing. I was invincible.

I'd heard that the nuns used rulers on the kids in their classes, so I figured that's what I was about to get. The priest grabbed my arm and led me to the front, right in front of the crucifix. *Bring it on*, I thought.

"Lay down." he boomed. "Nose to the floor."

*Here it comes.*

"Stretch your arms out."

*Just do it already.*

"Now stay there."

I heard the priest's footsteps, but with my nose to the floor I couldn't see where he was going. I lifted my head to look.

"Nose to the floor, Mr. Ridley." His voice echoed throughout the room, filling every nook and cranny of space for seconds after he had finished yelling.

I put my nose to the floor, my face burning. But I didn't move. It was the only dignity I had left, to keep from getting scolded by a man who believed in fairy tales.

I imagined the kids all snickering and laughing to each other. I imagined them saying, "Floyd finally met his match," and my face burned even hotter. Who did this priest think he was anyways?

After what felt like hours, the class was over. "You are dismissed," the priest said. "And that includes you, Mr. Ridley," he added as he walked toward the door connecting our classroom to the priest's quarters. "You may get up now."

The door creaked open and then clicked shut.

I got up quickly and grabbed my things from my seat, and ran home, avoiding everyone in my path.

When I walked in the door, my father was taking dinner out of the oven. "How was Catholic school?" he asked, not looking up. "You learn anything?"

"I learned that the terrazzo tile smells and that church doesn't do enough to keep it clean." I turned to storm up the stairs to my room, but a rough hand grabbed my arm.

"And just why do you know that?"

I pursed my lips and brushed away his hand. "The stupid priest made me lay on it, right in front of the crucifix for the whole class just because I made one joke."

Whether my father was drunk in that moment or not, he reacted like I said the priest had condemned me to hell himself. Within minutes we were in the car, headed back to the church.

"Stay in the car," he ordered. I nodded, cracking my window a few inches so I could hear what was about to happen. My father stomped up the door to the priest's home and knocked loudly.

"Hello?" I heard the muffled voice of the priest call through the door.

My father responded. "You'd better stay on the other side of that door, cause I'll knock you over so fast you won't know what hit you."

"Sir?"

"You heard me! I'll knock you out!" My father was stomping

and swinging his fisted hands as he yelled. "You never, *never, ever* do that to my son in front of his peers again! You had no right!" My father continued, adding in some colorful language as he reached the apex of his speech.

The priest didn't say anything else as far as I could hear. My father muttered a few things as he turned around and stormed back to the car. He sat in the driver's seat breathing heavily for a few moments, regaining his composure.

"Forget the priest. Forget the class," he said, putting the car into gear. "You don't have to go back there anymore—I don't care what your mother says. No priest is going to embarrass any son of mine."

And that was the last we spoke of it. My father dropped me off at home and then drove off to the bar to get my mother. I figured he decided to try to drink away his anger while he was there, and I wished I could have gone with him.

I guess maybe you can understand why the first day I got rip-roaring drunk on a bottle of wine was both a good day and a bad day. It was the day I finally found my escape, and it was the day I found my prison. Somehow, that day, at thirteen years old, I knew I was going to be an alcoholic.

What choice did I have? I definitely wasn't going to stop drinking. How could I? If I stopped, I'd have to think about how I would never be smart enough to make my teachers happy. I'd have to think about how long it would be before my brothers and I had to go through the garbage cans by the church for their leftovers because we were just that hungry. I'd have to think about how long it would be before our luck ran out and Dad came in and beat us again.

My life was like the kind of life you only saw in movies. Not the funny movies that families all watch together, but the kind of movies designed to make you cry. The kind of movies that should make you hug your kids a little tighter and pray a little harder. But alcohol had turned my life from a tragedy to a comedy, and I knew I'd be a fool to turn back.

# 2

## 1957

SHORTLY AFTER the day that I drank my first bottle of wine, my buddies and I started a gang. It started with me and my friend Rossy. He had an alcoholic mother too, so we ran together.

I once had other friends, friends who had nice mothers who knew how to cook and clean and showered their kids with hugs and kisses. I used to love to sit at the table and eat good food with them and play in their recreation rooms. It was the only place that I had to go. But by the time I was thirteen, those parents began to tell their kids not to hang around me.

Maybe they noticed that my clothes never seemed to get fully clean, or they heard about the fights I had in school, or they ran into my mother when she was blackout drunk. Whatever the reason, it drove me and Rossy together and we started spending time at his house because he had a TV. Some days, I would go there after school, and late at night, I would fall asleep on his couch. Neither of our parents cared, just so long as we weren't causing them trouble.

Then we started pitching in to buy wine together, and we shared whatever we had. We heard about the gangs in New York City, how everyone respected them and no one messed with them. They always had each other's backs, and they always had enough booze and food to go around. So, we decided that we would start our own, right there in Milford, Pennsylvania. We recruited about half a dozen guys, and we called ourselves the Black Widows. The black widow spiders were deadly, and we were so egotistical that we thought we were deadly too.

We hung out together pretty much all the time, whether we were supposed to be in school or not. Usually we'd spend our time smoking and drinking, but when our stash was running low we broke into stores and stole cartons of cigarettes. We thought we were being smart about it because we never broke into state stores, where we could get in trouble with the federal government if we got caught. We always robbed the small stores and bars, when we knew we could get away with it. We never got caught.

That's not to say we never got in trouble with the police. I was escorted home by the cops several times. Not that I ever wanted to cause them trouble specifically. In fact, I liked the police. Sometimes I laid in bed at night and made up stories about being a state trooper, because they were so sharp. I thought about being a state trooper and saving people. If I could be like them, women would love me, and people would respect me and think I was good looking.

But every time I looked in a mirror, that dream was ruined. I was skinny, with rotting teeth, and no hope of even getting a high school diploma. If there ever was a hopeless cause, I figured it was me.

That night, they escorted me to the door of my house and knocked loudly. My dad answered the door with a puzzled, half-drunken look on his face. "Floyd, what are you doing with these guys?"

"Mr. Ridley?"

"Yeah?" My dad grabbed my hand and pulled me inside. I didn't mind because it meant I definitely wasn't going to jail. At least, not that night.

"You'd better do something about Floyd and his behavior. We caught him fighting again, and if you don't do something, he's going to end up in jail." Their uniforms looked impressive, even slightly intimidating. I looked at their shiny buttons and stern faces. They didn't have to earn respect. Everyone always respected them.

Well, except my father. A normal father might have taken the police seriously, but whether it was because he was drunk, naive or stupid, my father didn't care.

"He'll outgrow it," he said. "Now get off my property." He stared at the cops until finally, they tipped their hats and walked down the porch steps to their car.

"Now you," he said, turning to me, "Get upstairs before I decide I should discipline you."

I turned and ran up the stairs and joined my younger two brothers in our bedroom.

"Is he mad?" Richie asked.

"Of course, he's mad," said Robert. "Floyd got brought home by the police again." He turned to me. "But how mad?"

I shrugged. I knew what they were asking. Was Dad going to come upstairs with belt in hand and go at it, or was he going to go to bed without bothering us?

"I think we're okay. You guys get in bed. I'll wait for him to go to bed before I go to sleep, okay?"

We were used to this routine of watching and waiting. Oftentimes, my dad and my mother came home yelling. I could never figure out what seemed to make them so mad. They could have been yelling about the color of the sky and I don't think it would have made a difference.

When that happened, my two younger brothers and I laid on our single mattress and listened to them yell. We hoped and prayed that Dad wouldn't come into our room, that they both would just go to bed, that we wouldn't have to wait for them to stop so we could fall asleep, that we wouldn't have to check for visible bruises before we went out anywhere the next day.

Every night was something different. Sometimes when he came home, he would be angry and start yelling at us. Yelling usually turned into hitting. I didn't mind so much when it was me he was hitting, but I couldn't take it when he would try to hit one of my brothers or my mother. Eyes blazing, drunk with rage at nothing in particular, Dad would take off his belt and raise it to hit my brothers and I would jump in front of him and try to fight him off. He was stronger than me, but I didn't mind. As long as he left them alone, I could handle it. I often listened to their feet run up the stairs to the safety of our bedroom while cuts and bruises burst through the surface of my skin.

My brothers looked at me with quiet admiration. I nodded my head toward our bed, and they slipped under the covers. I was still buzzed with alcohol, so I didn't mind that my dad might still come up and try to beat me. I didn't mind that I had to try to be the protector of two little boys.

# 3

## 1959

I WAS SIXTEEN when I got put on probation. The court didn't want me to stay with my parents during that time, so my sister offered to take me in. She lived in the country in a beautiful house that her husband had built for her and her six kids. She was a night nurse at a local nursing home, so my job was to get the kids bathed and in bed, then get them up for school in the morning. Then when she came home, she went to sleep, and I watched the kids that were too young to go to school.

I was there for two years like that, and I liked it because it was a nice home to live in. It wasn't like the ghetto where I was. She got me nice clothes and she fed me well.

Her husband, a carpenter, was an alcoholic too. But much like our father, he always went to work early in the morning. We got along OK until one evening when he came home late from the bar.

I was watching TV like I usually did after the kids went to bed. He came in and sat down next to me. I could smell the alcohol on him because he was sitting very close. Then he took his hand and put it on my leg. For a moment, I felt frozen. He started rubbing my leg, up and down.

"Don't do that," I said. But he kept rubbing back and forth. Then he moved to grabbing me. I quickly pushed him off and stood up. "I'm going to tell my sister," I said.

"No, you won't. I'll shoot you," he replied. The look in his eyes said that he wasn't lying, so I ran upstairs and went to bed. Some time later, I woke up, feeling cold and exposed. Suddenly, I realized that he had pulled away the sheets and pulled off my underwear. I couldn't get away. I was stuck. Trapped.

Fear turned into adrenaline and I started fighting, pushing, doing anything I could to get him to stop. I felt his calloused hand hit me across the back. I shoved his body away from mine. Another hit came across my face. Did I taste blood? It didn't matter. I pressed him again, with as much strength as I had in my 100 pound body and finally I was free.

We stared at each other in the dark for a moment, our chests both heaving, mine with excess adrenaline and relief, and his with frustration. He stared at me a moment longer, his eyes narrowing, before he turned and sulked back to his room.

In the morning, after he left for work, I told my sister what had happened. She told me that she wanted to file for divorce and called a state cop that she knew. "I want him arrested for molesting my brother," she told him.

We found out later that he had done it to his stepson too. They threw him in jail, but he got out. He was on a restraining order, but he tried to come by the house anyways. I used to sit in front of the front door with a .22-caliber rifle. I told myself that if he ever walked in the door, I would shoot him. Fortunately, he never came in.

Besides that incident, I enjoyed the two years that I spent with my sister. Sure, I missed hanging out with my friends, but she had plenty of wine that I could drink in the cellar, and her house was warm, safe, and full of food. But once the probation was over, I went right back to Milford and my old gang.

It was like nothing had changed. We went right back to stealing, fighting, and drinking. And I knew that they all had my back. That was the best thing about being in a gang. I didn't have to worry about anyone taking advantage of me or hurting me. Someone always had my back. And I feared the day where that wouldn't be the case. What little alcohol couldn't do for me, friends did.

The thing about alcohol and the company of friends was that they made me do things I normally wouldn't do. We would frequently drink together and then go out and rob a local business. It was nothing big or serious—we figured it was just a small nuisance to the businessmen, a few bucks here, a few bucks there.

Besides, we never wanted to risk getting into any real trouble. For all the bad things we did, we knew that we did not want to end up in jail.

In fact, before I went to jail, I had little knowledge of it. I didn't know about how the inmates could make their own alcohol if they were smart enough and sneaky enough to do it. I didn't know how your image was more important than anything else, because if you looked like you could be bullied, you would be. But I had heard of gang rapes, and I had heard of men getting stabbed with sharpened toothbrushes, and I had heard of men going in for a short sentence and never coming out again.

So when, after getting picked up by the police for robbing

a man's house with my gang, I found myself faced with the choice between going into the military and jail, the answer was obvious. Who in their right mind would choose prison anyways?

I told the judge my choice, my voice reflecting an unusual degree of respect. I didn't want to be myself and accidentally lose the option of going into the military. The judge nodded, clearly not really caring about the outcome of my case, and banged his gavel in agreement.

# 1962

I SET OUT for basic training in 1962. I had to lie about my birthday because I was technically only seventeen years old when I signed up.

I know the judge intended it as a punishment, but I found that I quite liked the military. Of course, I wasn't able to have alcohol, on account of my being underage, but the inconvenience of sneaking it on base was a small price to pay.

As it turns out, I was a good soldier. I could run fast, and I liked the rhythm and routine of military life. Never in my life had I had my own bed, clean clothes, and three meals to eat every single day. And all they wanted me to do in return was exercise and follow orders. They even paid me seventy-three dollars a month! A small price to pay indeed.

After I finished basic training, they started giving us weekend passes so we could go off base and spend some time with friends or family. As soon as training was done on Friday, I bolted off base just as fast as I could. The nearest bar was a few towns away, and when I arrived on Sunday afternoon, I knew I couldn't stay long. But once the alcohol started surging through my bloodstream, nothing else really mattered. The military, the judge, my brother-in law, my drunk parents. Everything seemed to melt away as I lived in the laughter and glow of my oldest and best friend. I stayed at the bar until eleven, twelve, one o'clock in the morning before the bartender finally convinced me to leave.

Someone drove me back and I passed sheepishly through the checkpoints, ready to get an earful, but they just let me sign in and go straight to barracks. The next morning, I received word that our commanding officer wanted to see me. He was an intimidating man, if only for his size and his title. He sat behind a big wooden desk waiting for me. His uniform inspired respect, just like the police uniforms.

I wish that I could say I learned my lesson, but I didn't. In fact, I hardly ever came back on time. I had kitchen duty a few times. Other times, they would make me stay on base for a few weekends in a row, making me clean bathrooms and work in the kitchen while my friends and fellow soldiers were out living the high life.

When I couldn't leave, I would find a way to get alcohol onto the base.

You would get extra duty if you got caught, but for me, it was worth it. I hid a pint in my extra pair of combat boots in my locker. It was my nature to get in trouble, whether for alcohol or fighting or something entirely unrelated. It was all I knew. I bent the rules thinking that I could get away with it. When I was drunk, I believed I *would* get away with it! And when I got caught, I would just promise myself that I would be more careful.

It turned into a cycle. Every day I tried a new way to beat the system, but they were always one step ahead of me.

And I had friends. Not great friends. Not lifelong friends, but I had friends in the sense that I knew that I would never be on my own as long as I was in the military. No matter what enemy came our way, I would never be left alone to face them. The military, for that time, was my new gang. A band of brothers dedicated to life, liberty, and pursuit of happiness.

After I was finished with my basic training, I was assigned to serve the remainder of my six-year commitment in the Army Reserves, based in Strasbourg, just a few miles from Milford and my old gang. I still got paid every month, but I got to live off base, have another job, and most importantly, drink.

During the week I held a menial job in construction. I would spend my days mixing and hauling cement always looking forward to the weekend, when I would travel to New York. There, the drinking age was eighteen. I wasn't really eighteen, but the fake ID that my gang had given me was a pretty good one, and soon enough I turned eighteen and could get in with my real ID.

And then I began that old familiar pattern.

What was the point of having a job anyways? What was the point of mixing and hauling cement all day long? "They're working us to death!" I'd say to another worker, or a bartender, or a friend. "And for what? A measly three twenty-five an hour."

Then my hand would find a cool glass of booze, and with one gulp, even the frustration and menial nature of the job didn't matter.

"You'll get something better," they replied.

"Yeah." Another sip, another gulp. "I'm gonna make it big, and when I do, I'll be telling everyone about you and the conversations that we had. Maybe, I'll be a movie star, or a guitar player." I could see myself on stage, or walking into a movie premiere, dressed in the sharpest suit that money could buy, a beautiful girl on my arm. I'd be able to have anything and everything that I wanted. "Maybe, by then, I'll finally quit drinking."

The sound of an empty glass on a wood table top jerked me out of my daydream. "Another, please."

The money was the only reason that I worked as long as I did, but even that couldn't keep me faithful to the job. At first, I would be just a little late, then a few hours late, and finally, there were days that I didn't show up to work at all.

Then, one day I woke up thinking that there was an earthquake or something. My bed was shaking so violently that I thought for sure something was wrong. When I went to steady myself, I realized that it wasn't the bed that was shaking. It was me and I couldn't stop.

Everything shook violently. My heart raced. My thoughts raced. Nothing would stop or stand still. I tried to look for a bottle of whisky, beer, anything to get my mind off the terrible betrayal of my own body.

I learned later that these were called delirium tremens, or DTs, as they're often called. DTs happen when people stop drinking alcohol. The doctors actually told me never to try to quit cold turkey, because the DTs would kill me. For that reason, I kept a bottle by my bed so I would never have a chance of going into withdrawal.

Of all the things I faced in my life, withdrawal was one of the things that scared me the most. The shakes were one thing, but the visions and the hallucinations, and the dreadful mixture of the reality of my condition and the dreams and visions, which seemed so real, was more than I was willing to take.

Another night at the bar, I looked at my buddies, the Black Widows, talking and laughing, and the night grew later and later. Most of the working men had left already. I'd checked the clock behind the bar several times already, trying to decide how late I could push it.

"You're looking nervous, Floyd. Got someone to meet?" one of them called.

The group laughed. "Who you waiting for at almost one in the morning."

"Ah, shut up. You know I have work in the morning."

"Yeah, yeah, like that usually matters."

"Hey, how come none of you are lookin' at the clock?"

Suddenly, it dawned on me that my friends had somehow outsmarted the system, they had outsmarted the way of life that so many adults stand by. "How are you getting money to come out here every night?"

The boys shared a laugh and a wry look between them when the one sitting closest to me leaned over and said, "We've got our ways. Don't you worry about us."

I laughed. "Worry about you? No. Seriously. Tell me what your secret is."

One of my buddies looked over to see how close the bartender was. "You really wanna know?"

"I really wanna know."

"Fine." He inched even closer. "We have a little crime ring going, like back when we was all in Milford."

"You're stealing?"

"Yeah. Don't be too loud about it. We've got room for you, if you're still interested."

Was I still interested? I left my wallet, knowing that I probably wasn't going to make much money from my job. Heck. They'd probably fire me before the month was up. And then what?

"I'm in. What's the next job?"

They partnered me up with one of the guys and we robbed a convenience store the next night. The guys had figured out a way to get in and out with some money without getting caught. And they still didn't steal from anywhere that would be a federal offense.

When we divided up the money, I kept half of it and put the rest in a safety deposit box in Manhattan. I knew I would need the money later, because at that rate, it wasn't a question of *if* I was going to get fired. It was a question of *when*. Every time I did a job, I took what I needed off the top and saved the rest.

I would sit at the bar all day, talking with everyone that came in. I wouldn't have to leave at all to go home, except when the bartender decided it was time for everyone to go home, or at least get out.

One night, I decided to a solo job. A big engineering firm. Through the grapevine, I found out it had a big safe, and luckily for me, I was great at cracking safes. It was dark, late, and cool. The leaves were just starting to change, and they crunched beneath my feet. I didn't worry about the noise because nobody was there. Besides, my only thought was on the money and how long it would last me. Probably a month, maybe more.

I broke in the back door, picked the lock, and made my way to the safe.

I grabbed the cool lock on the safe and began turning it, waiting for those almost-silent clicks. Right... tick. Left... tick. Right... tick. My pulse picked up a little with excitement. Wait till the boys saw the prize I got from this one. I tried to guess how much money there would be inside. A few hundred at least, and if I was lucky, maybe several thousand. Rich.

I swung the safe open and looked inside. It was dark, too dark to really see, but it looked empty. I put my hand on the bottom in the center. Empty. I swept my hand side to side, excitement now to turning to anger.

Where was it? I felt all around the safe, looking for a stack of bills in every corner, even stuck to the top. Nothing. I had been tricked. Outsmarted by people one step ahead of me, as they always were.

I slammed the safe shut and sat in front of it for a moment. How could I have been this stupid? How could I have come to rob a place that had nothing for me to rob? Did they know?

I froze. Did they? How could they know?

Maybe they knew all along. Maybe the cops knew all along. I had been running with the Black Widows for a few months. Maybe our time was up.

"They're going to catch you Floyd." I said out loud to myself. "They're going to catch you and this time you won't even be able to take a deal and go with the military. You'll probably never get to go to the military again, period, after they hear about this."

I tried to think clearly and logically about it all, but I was still drunk from what I had had earlier in the night.

"Who do you call?" I asked myself. "Where do you go?" I couldn't go to any of my friends. If I was found out, so were they, I figured. And I couldn't go home.

Finally, I settled on calling a guy named Matt. He had been really good friends with my father, and he was a state trooper. It seemed like the best option, considering the circumstances. I found a phone and dialed his number.

Matt answered. "Hello?"

"Hey Matt. It's Floyd Ridley."

"Floyd." Was he surprised? Was he expecting me? His voice didn't give any clues. "How can I help you?"

"I'm the guy you're looking for," I said.

"What do you mean?" he asked.

"I'm your boy. I'm the one you've been trying to catch." Maybe, I figured, if they hadn't caught the rest of the gang, I could, at least, be the hero.

"Well, then, why don't you come on down to the station?"

"I'll need a ride. I'm outside Hausser Engineering."

Fifteen minutes later a black car came and took me down to the station. They put me in a small room and interrogated me, asking me everything about the crimes that I had committed. I told them everything I could, but I did my best to keep the rest of the Black Widows out of it.

"You're sure no one else helped you?" the officer said.

"Positive, sir. It was just me."

"Well, that's funny," he said as he stood up and walked around his chair. "Because we have some of your buddies in the other room, and they say that you all did them together. No doubt, you did some of these on your own, but you don't have anyone to protect. We already know it all."

As it turned out, my buddies had been caught the night before, doing a different job. The police had had eyes on me anyways. They said that they knew I was involved when they picked up the rest of the Black Widows. After all, I was the one who had brought the gang together in the first place.

"So now what?"

"Well, Floyd," they said, "we've got you on crimes in three different states, New York, New Jersey, and Pennsylvania. You'll be charged here first, and from what I've just heard it should be a short case. Then, once you've done your time here, there's going to be a detainer on you, so you're going to go away for a long time."

The man left me to sit alone in the room for a little while before they took me to a holding cell.

In a week or so, I had a visitor. The Army had sent a man over. I stood up at attention. "Sir."

"At ease, Ridley. You're not in the Army anymore." He

passed me a packet of papers, turned and left. The army never was much for speeches or fond goodbyes. I held the papers in my hand. Worst case scenario was a dishonorable discharge. I knew that. Best case, maybe they fake the numbers a little and call it a medical discharge. I opened the papers hoping for anything but a dishonorable.

Undesirable Discharge. I had done all right in the Army, but since I couldn't keep my act together, they figured it was in their best interest to wash their hands of me. A lot of people would want to do that now, I figured. I hadn't seen my father or any of my brothers since I'd been arrested. A few weeks later—with no friends, no family, and no fellow gang of freedom fighters—I started my 6-year sentence.

I had managed to avoid prison for the first nineteen years of my life, but as they transported me there, I wondered if I would make it out. Maybe I was vain, but I thought of myself as an attractive, if skinny, young man, vulnerable prey to the various derelicts of prison life. All the rumors that I had heard came flooding back to me, gang rape, self-made weapons, untold challenges.

We arrived at the gates.

The first prison was for young offenders, since I was not technically twenty years old. I spent the first week by myself. They called it "adjusting to prison life." This was quarantine. They know you won't last if you get put in a cell right away. If the gangs don't get you, shock will.

I had just gone from being free to do what I wanted, when I wanted, with no consequences or a life of rules and orders. And unlike with the Army, I wasn't getting paid, and there was no such thing as weekend leave.

# NOVEMBER 1962

I WAS SCARED. Almost as scared as when my brother-in-law came at me, but not quite. That was a fear for the safety of my body, the fear of being abused and damaged. Sitting alone in my cell, I didn't care about my body. I cared for my life, my sanity. I knew that over the next six years, everything would be on the line.

"Six years?"

I swore under my breath. "God, I'm gonna die. I'm gonna die here." The thought repeated in my mind, *I would die here.* Nineteen years old with a scrawny body like mine? I would be lucky if I lasted six months.

The thought of my own death overwhelmed me. I was cute, and from what I had heard, they loved cute boys in prison. It was like I was back at my sister's house with her husband coming at me. Only this time, there were ten of him.

I could see myself fighting him off. I could see myself being beaten, barely recognizable. Bones breaking through muscle and skin. I could hear myself yelling, begging for them to stop, and the world going black. I saw my funeral. Would my father come? My mother? In my mind, I couldn't see the seats—just the plain, wooden coffin and my own lifeless body. Dead.

A strangled yell echoed down the hall to my ears, bringing me back to reality, scaring the thought of death away. No, death wasn't an option. I just had to survive six years. But what if? No. If someone tried to mess with me, I decided that I was going to have to kill him.

A few days later, I got word from some guys who I had known on the streets. They were Gorillas and, as luck would have it, they were in the cell I was assigned to, K-block cell.

"Tell Floyd not to worry about when he gets into general population. We'll take care of him," their message said. Their words were some comfort, but what I really needed was some liquid courage.

I got my work assignment after being there a day or two. It was down in the laundry.

Being in general population was just as bad as everyone had told me it was. Every day, it seemed that there was a new story. Someone was raped, someone was stabbed, someone was sent to the infirmary. Sometimes I knew them. Sometimes I got lucky and didn't know them.

When you didn't know the guys, it was just scary. When you knew them, you knew how close you were to being the one they went after. For example, my friend Bobby. I hadn't seen him in a day or two. "Where's Bobby been? He get put in isolation again?"

"Nah, he got jumped in the factory. Gang of eight guys overpowered him. They each had to take a turn."

"He comin' back?"

"Not sure man, he looked pretty rough. I think they had to take him to the hospital."

In prison, you didn't have the chance to be a nice guy. You had to be rough. You had to prove that you were the wrong person to mess with. One day, I was going back to my cell and a guy jumped me. He was trying to attack me so I grabbed his shirt and shoved him toward the railing so I could pin him. By the time I got to the railing, we had so much momentum that he tipped over the railing. I let go and watched the man fall three stories down, landing on his back.

Inside I was screaming. I was crying. I was trying to find a way to fix it. I never wanted to kill anyone. It was a sure way to stay in prison forever. I just wanted to be safe. But everyone was watching. So instead of breaking down, instead of running off or staring in disbelief, I muttered, "He had it coming," and walked off to my cell. Some of the newer guys stared at me with wide eyes.

People standing between me and my cell moved apart. I was like Moses parting the Red Sea, except instead of being a hero, I was a villain.

I chugged the last of my current stash of booze, hid the bottle and opened a book. There was no doubt that they were going to search us all after what had just happened. My hands were shaking. The words seemed to dance all over the page.

I heard the guards running through the prison. "Out of the way! Get a stretcher and get the doctor down here!"

Their boots were always loud, but, as they ran now the noises pounded into my brain. Everyone saw me do it—no doubt about that. They'd be coming for me soon.

"Everybody back in your cells," one guard started yelling. A few minutes later the buzzer went off and the doors closed. I kept my eyes glued to my book.

We stayed inside our cells for a long time. For a while, there was a lot of noise as the guards and doctors tried to deal with what had happened, but slowly the noises died off.

It was getting late when, finally, the officers started making rounds. "You see anything?" they asked. They spent more time with some criminals than others. Finally, a middle-aged officer rapped on my door. "Come here, you," he said.

I rolled out of bed and walked over to him.

"You know anything about what just happened?" His voice was stern. It had to be. Criminals were rough guys.

"No sir," I said. "I didn't see nothin."

The cop locked eyes with me and stared so hard his eyes scrunched together. We held each other's gaze in a game of chicken. I wasn't bending first. I couldn't. Finally, he broke his gaze and sharply turned to the right to continue his investigation.

I waited for the cops to come back to my cell all night, but when it was time for breakfast, no one had returned. So, I went to breakfast. I went to work. I went to dinner. Still, no one came, and they never did.

I don't know if the guys just didn't want to mess with me, or if they just knew how much of a jerk the guy was who came after me. Either way, I was free.

Whenever I walked by, some of the guys would whisper, "He's crazy." But I didn't mind. It kept them off my back.

I survived prison the only way I knew how: thoroughly and completely drunk. When you're desperate, you'll do anything. And I already knew I couldn't be sober long without memories and fears and reality flooding into my mind in the most overwhelming way.

So, my buddies and I would smuggle sugar, yeast and grains from the kitchen. I found a small, hidden place on the lower level of the prison and brewed it there. Guys would trade me cartons of cigarettes for a drink. It was like our own little society. Everyone had something that they could make and sell or trade. We all stayed drunk. Some guys stayed high. We were just surviving.

It wasn't all terrible. For one, I learned that I actually *wasn't* stupid. All my life, my teachers and my parents had told me that I was. Imagine living twenty years on Earth and the first time that someone tells you that you have potential is in a jail cell schoolroom.

They offered free GED classes to convicts. I guess that they wanted us to better ourselves or see our own potential. I only went because it meant that I could get out of my cell. We learned grammar, science, and history; my favorite was reading.

Every day, the library cart would roll by my cell and I'd trade in the books that I had read for some new ones. All told, I think I read thousands of books in prison. When I didn't know what a word meant, I'd look it up. I then looked for an opportunity to use it. I would confuse a guy out in the yard, impress a friend during meal times; I did whatever worked.

And so, I learned that I could, in fact, *learn* just like everyone else. In a way, I wished my teachers could see me. I wished that they could see how wrong they had been about me and see how their words had hurt and frustrated me. I wished that I could show them how wrong they were to give up on me.

I did get out twice. Once was on parole. They told me that I could go free as long as I didn't do any drinking. Well, I was back in within the week. Some rat called my parole officer the moment I stepped foot in a bar. I had had enough of fake booze and drinking things that human beings were never meant to drink.

Maybe I should have been more careful, waited a week or so before I went out. Maybe it wouldn't have mattered at all. Even so, I was right back in jail.

My second trip was shorter and much less fun.

"Hey you," I heard a guard call. "Chaplain needs to see you."

"Chaplain?" I asked, moving cautiously toward the door. I certainly had never spoken to the chaplain, and he had certainly never spoken to me before.

"Don't get smart; just get moving." The officer let me out of my cell and cuffed me for the walk to the chaplain's office.

He was a nice enough looking man. He had old eyes that almost seemed permanently sad except for a little sparkle when he said something that he thought was exceptionally spiritual.

Next to him stood our warden. *An odd combination*, I thought to myself, still wondering what was going on.

"Have a seat, Floyd," the chaplain said. I slowly did. I watched him close and tried to read him.

"I have some bad news, son," he said. "We just got word that your mother has passed away." He paused. "She's dead, son."

I slowly nodded and processed the information. Was I supposed to be crying? My eyes felt a little wet, but I hardly felt anything inside.

"I'm sure this comes as a shock to you." Another long pause. I nodded slowly. He did say *dead*, didn't he? Still no tears.

This time it was the warden who spoke. "Two marshals are coming to pick you up and they'll take you to your mother's funeral and then bring you back. Is that something you want to do?"

I thought for a moment. Visit my mother's funeral? What kind of son would I be if I didn't go? What kind of son would I be if I did? "Yeah, I'll go," I finally answered.

They gave me a suit to wear and helped me fix my hair and face before loading me into the back of a transport car. I remember getting to the funeral home in handcuffs. The cuffs were mostly hidden under the baggy arms of my suit, but the awkward position of my arms and the two uniformed marshals on either side of me were dead giveaways. No, Floyd was not a free man.

My brother Arty met us outside. It was clear that he was running the show as usual. He always managed to keep his life together. "Can you take those cuffs off?" he asked one of the guards. "There's a lot of people here and he has to go in and see his mother."

The guard narrowed his eyes and looked at me and said, "You make one false move and I'll blow you away."

"I'm not going anywhere sir," I said.

I walked down the aisle to my mother's coffin. Her body looked lifeless. *Was* lifeless. They had put her in a nice dress and someone had fixed her hair and makeup. I had seen dead people before and they never looked like themselves. She really *didn't* look like herself. I paused a moment trying to remember what she looked like when I had last seen her, and I couldn't do it. To my shame, I couldn't remember what my mother looked like in real life.

I looked at Arty, who stood beside me. "I don't even know that woman."

I felt a hand on my shoulder and as I turned around, a rough hand slapped my face. *Smack!* "You heartless..." He swore at me. Were those tears in his eyes? The crowd of people looked at us, helpless and shocked. I touched my face, took one last look at my mom, then turned toward the marshals.

"I'm ready," I said. And the two men escorted me out the door and back into the transport van, back to prison. All told, I think that I was out only a few hours, but it felt like I had never really left.

In 1965, prison life got a little more interesting. Some law had passed called the Miranda Act and guys were being taken back to court and released because they had improper counsel. One guy, William Walsh—we called him William the Worm—was in for killing nine people. He got freed under that Miranda thing. The day that he got out, I said to him, "You killed them. You killed those nine people, didn't you?"

William smiled a wry smile. "Yes, I did." He smiled a bit more. "And now I'm going to go kill some more."

I was angry. I had no chance of getting out under the Miranda Act since I had admitted my guilt, yet William killed nine people and got to walk out a free man. And this is supposed to be the justice system? Killers, rapists, child molesters, all of them got turned loose. Five hundred guys in total got out because of that Miranda Act.

Now, a lot of them came back. Some of them even got the Habitual Criminal Act. That was when you got caught doing the same crime three times. Get caught raping or stealing or fighting, you didn't get five to ten again. No, you got put in for life.

That was one of the things that scared me. Prison life was so rough and unpredictable that I promised myself that I would never go back to prison. As I left the prison cell on November 22, 1969, my time was done. I said to myself, "Maybe I'll go back to jail for drinking or fighting, but there's no way I'm going back to prison. I will never come back here."

I stepped out of the gates and breathed in my first breath of air as a free man in six years. A black car pulled up to the prison gate. I wondered who had come to take me home. Dad? Definitely not. One of the Black Widows? Probably not. They were all still doing time. Arty? Maybe. But he had seemed too angry with me at the funeral.

As the car got closer I saw them: Government plates.

A large, muscular man with a mean looking faced stepped out of the van. "We'll take it from here, gentlemen," he said to the two guards who had been standing just a few paces behind me. Then he looked at me. "Mr. Ridley, New Jersey would like a word with you."

There are few things as dramatic or as frustrating as having freedom and then having it snatched out from under you. I was led into the back of the car and handcuffed again. The whole way from Pittsburgh to New Jersey, I thought about going back to jail in a new state with new inmates. People who didn't know me. People who had no reason to protect me. I had been promising myself for the last six years that, no matter what, I wouldn't go back to jail, and now I was on my way without even having a chance to prove that I had changed.

I had to hang around a few days and wait for the judge to see me. When I finally did, he was an imposing man. His face said that he was tired of excuses, tired of people failing him over and over.

"I ought to give you 15 years, son," he said without even looking at me.

"Yes, sir," I said.

"But I have here a letter from an officer over in Pittsburgh, Pennsylvania."

My eyes darted up. "Sir?"

"He's recommended leniency." He looked down at a letter, creased from being shoved in an envelope. "Says that you did your time and you've never given anyone trouble since. Is this true?"

"Yes, sir."

The judge contorted his face for a moment, weighing his options, deciding what judgment he would give me, what future he would give me. "I'm willing to rule in favor of probation, on one condition."

"Anything," I said.

"You are not to set foot in the state of New Jersey ever again, Mr. Ridley."

I held back a smile. "I won't even fly over your state, your honor."

The judge tapped his gavel, cementing his decision, and I could breathe again. But my joy was short-lived because as I stepped off the courthouse steps, there was another black van with two more US marshals waiting for me. New York wanted to have its turn to hand down justice.

The New York judge said, "So, you've been to jail already in Pennsylvania?"

"Yes, I have. Six years."

The judged nodded, with a look of satisfaction. "Tell you what I'm gonna do here. You got any savings?"

"Yes, your honor."

"You have enough to cover the money you stole?"

I thought back to all the money that I had added to my safety deposit box, the money I had hoped to use to start a new life and a new way of living.

"I think so."

"You pay restitution for everything you stole, and I think we have ourselves a deal."

I hesitated. All my money in exchange for freedom. All my hopes for a fresh start.

"Do we have a deal?"

Better free and broke than back in prison, I thought. "Yes, your honor."

The gavel banged. I breathed a sigh of relief. They handed me a letter saying that I was free to go, and then led me out the courthouse steps.

I turned and looked behind me and, for the first time, the guards had all returned to their posts. There was no black car waiting for me and no warrants out for my arrest. All I had was the suit on my back and forty dollars in my pocket, but I was free.

No one could look at me and know that I was a convicted felon, at least, not right away. No one was going to make me check in with them, or strip-search me, or keep me from smoking a cigarette. For the first time, in a long time, I felt shame lift off of me.

Then it fell back on me like a ton of bricks. I had nowhere to go, no one to turn to. No job, no apartment, no nothing. I found a pay phone and played with the cord while I thought of who to call. My dad? Probably not after the incident at the funeral. My buddies were still in jail, and probably didn't have any money to let me borrow anyways. Finally, I settled on Arty.

Arty was always the best brother to me, to everyone. I used to get mad at him because he was so good at everything. I walked to what looked like a main road and waited for a car to pass by so I could hitchhike.

Arty was handsome and athletic, much more athletic than the rest of us. Growing up, it always seemed like his name was in the paper—for good things. When I started school, before I had the reputation of being a fighter, I had the reputation of being Arty's brother. All the teachers wanted me to be just like him, and when they found out I was just a daydreamer with half a brain, well, let's just say that they didn't try to hide their disappointment. And maybe, I was a little disappointed too.

Let's face it, no younger brother likes being compared to his older brother. Usually, it's not because they don't *want* to live up to their reputation; it's because they're worried they won't be able to. Sure, I fought and skipped school, but only after I gave up on trying. When you try and try for so long and everyone just gets disappointed, you figure it's easier to just let them be disappointed and stop killing yourself with the effort.

An average-looking car driven by an average looking man slowed down next to me. "Where you headed?" he asked. He didn't look suspicious of me at all. Probably because I was still in my suit from the court hearing. The lawyer made sure that I came in looking sharp.

"Milford, or anywhere close."

"I'm headed near there. Hop in."

"Thank you very much." I hopped in, carrying my few belongings and, for the first time in a long time, relaxed. I was safe.

# 4

## 1968

AFTER A FEW HOURS, we were in Milford, and I was able to walk to the law firm where I knew Arthur worked.

It was dark inside. It seemed stiff, just like the law offices in the movies. I walked up to an anxious-looking secretary sitting behind a large desk.

"Can I help you, sir?" she asked.

"Yeah, I'm here to see Arty," I said. The secretary's eyes flicked nervously to the office door to her right. "Tell him his brother Floyd is a free man."

"Absolutely. Let me see if he is available," she said picking up the telephone and punching a few numbers. "Mr. Ridley?" she said after a moment or two. "There's a man named Floyd here to see you. Says he's your brother." A pause. "Okay." She hung up the receiver and gave me a cautious smile. "He'll be out in a minute."

"Okay," I said, taking a step back.

A minute later the office door swung open and Arthur walked briskly toward me. "What do you want, Floyd?"

"What kind of hello is that?"

"You can't just come into my office when I'm working, Floyd."

"Well, I didn't know what else to do, who else to go to. Definitely not dad." Arty looked blankly at me, unsympathetic.

"Look, I just got out, and I need some help getting started with my life. I thought you could give me a hand." I smiled my best smile at him. "What do you say, Art?"

Arthur rubbed his head, pushing his hair off his forehead and messing it up a bit. "Come on Floyd. But you know you can't stay here."

"I can't?"

"No," he said. He shook his head and put his hands on his hips. "Come in here." I followed him into his office and he shut the door.

"Look Floyd, I'm sorry, but there really isn't anything more that I can do for you besides give you a little money. Everyone here thinks you're a crook, a no-good alcoholic. There's no possible future here." He reached into a desk drawer, counted out a few bills and then set them on the table. "Take it and go find a life—anywhere but here."

I wasn't shocked. Maybe I should have been. Normally, you wouldn't expect your own family to treat you like a con man, but I suppose my family wasn't a normal family, and my crimes were probably worse than those of most men my age. I nodded slowly and picked up the money.

"Thanks, brother," I said. I counted the money right there in front of him. "This will help. I appreciate your help."

"Floyd, you know that if I could…"

"It's fine, Art. I'll see you someday," I said as I opened the door and walked out of the office, head held high, heart beating fast, wondering how long it would take me to get out of town and find a bar.

# 5

## 1969

IN NO TIME, the money was gone. Fast. I thought I could manage it better, but in reality, I barely remember the things I bought. Some beer, then some new clothes, more beer, and then it was gone. I was in New York when I ran out of money, so I went to the only place that I knew I could learn how to survive: the Bowery, a.k.a. Skid Row.

It is odd that I thought of a place, that seemed surrounded by death and despair, as a place that could save me and teach me how to survive. Whether it was a good idea or not, it was the exact place that I headed. Even though its exact location was always changing, you could tell that it was coming for a few blocks. I kept crossing crosswalks expecting to see it, but each street seemed only marginally more inhabited by derelicts than the last, until suddenly I knew that I was there.

The streets of the Bowery were virtually lined with beggars and drunkards, each more sorry looking than the last. I probably looked like a college boy compared to the rest of the street. Hungry eyes looked at me as I walked past, hungry for food and hungry for my attention.

"Can you spare a dime?"

"Buy a drink for an army vet?"

"Want a good time?"

I kept walking, not yet ready to stop and try to make myself at home. I wandered into a bar and had a seat. I still had a little money, and besides, I thought better and more boldly when I was good and drunk.

"You new around here?" the guy next to me asked.

"Just checking things out."

"Don't stay too long," he laughed. "You hang around here too long and the only way that you'll leave is in a cardboard coffin."

I brushed off his words, not really in the mood to chat.

"Where you from?"

"Milford," I said, fixing my eyes on the bartender. "Whiskey please."

"You got it. And you," he said, pointing at the guy sitting next to me, "quit buggin' my customers."

The man next to me slumped a bit in his seat, finished his drink and walked out. I should have said, "Thank you," but my focus was on that drink and the clarity it would bring.

I didn't feel scared a whole lot at this point, but I knew when I was about to be scared. Fear always gripped me in a weird way. Some people say that it feels like being punched in the gut, but I say that it feels like the moment before you know that you're going to get punched in the gut. Your muscles tense too early because they're anticipating it and you can't get them to relax to take it like a man.

The bartender brought me my drink and courage filled my body in one gulp. I left some money on the table and went on to check out my new home.

I looked up and down the streets. The Bowery stretched on as far as I could see. People were everywhere. They lined the streets on either side. People were standing up drinking and sitting down smoking dope. Hands outstretched toward the passerby, hoping for a nickel or a dime. There were hundreds of people who were not living, yet not dying, at least, not yet. If I was one of them, did that I mean I was also neither living nor dying?

The first day was hard. The second day was harder. I had some experience with begging, hustling, and stealing, but I didn't have enough experience to do much more than barely stay alive.

After a few days, I knew that I wasn't going to survive on my own, so I started asking around for help.

"Hey, who's been here the longest?" I asked one of the guys who was working the street corner across from the one I was begging at.

"Dunno," he said, brushing me off. "You don't know anybody?"

He turned his body away from me, focused on getting the last few cents he needed before he could get a new bottle.

"Pete," he said gruffly. "Now get outta my corner."

Pete. I hadn't heard of anyone called Pete, so I went down to one of the local restaurants and asked the cook as I ordered a 5-cent sandwich. "You know a Pete?"

"Pete who?"

"All I know is his name's Pete. A guy down the road told me

that he's lived here the longest."

"Oh, Panhandle Pete!"

"That's gotta be him," I said, hoping that it was in fact the man who I was looking for.

"He's usually down by the corner on the south side. Gray haired fellow with a beard."

"C'mon, that describes about fifty percent of the guys out here!" I protested.

"Sorry, but that's all I got. He's old. He's the oldest guy you'll see out here. Hope it helps."

I finished my sandwich and headed down to the south side to try to catch him before he disappeared for the night.

The cook was right. He was the oldest man that I had seen there. He must have been at least sixty years old and looked like he had lived a life that was even longer than that.

"Excuse me, sir. Are you, Panhandle Pete?"

The man laughed, the laughter breaking through the solemnity of his resting facial expression. "That's what they call me."

"Well, Pete...I could use your help." I looked around. "It looks like I'm going to be here for a while and I have no clue what to do."

For the next two years, Pete was my mentor. We would run together for the most part. He taught me how to hustle, every con trick in the book. He showed me where to find food, clothes, shelter, either cheap or totally free. He had been an engineer, up until he lost his wife and kids in a fire. After that, he lost everything he had, started drinking, and ended up on Skid Row. So, he decided to stay there and die there.

It's like elephants. When elephants know that they are going to die, they have a special place that they go to.

And people did die. Every day. Some died of overdoses,

some were murdered, some froze to death, and some just gave up. Every day people would come down Houston Street in a van. They would park in front of our buildings, go inside, and carry the bodies down the steps and into the van. It was the march and rhythm of the day. You woke up, hustled, found somewhere safe to sleep, and if you woke up in the morning, you did it all over again. I'm not sure how many bodies I saw come out of the buildings. Probably hundreds. Maybe even more.

I knew people who died like that. In fact, I only knew one person who didn't die like that. Boston Billy and I would work a hustle together and split the profits. One day, I told him that I had to go down to Lafayette and White for some errand, and when I got back, I found out that he was dead.

As I came back to the area, a man yelled for me. "Renegade! Hang on!"

I turned toward him, ready to run if I had to, one hand protecting my cash, the other ready to strike.

"You ran with Billy, right?"

I stared him down.

"Boston Billy?"

"Yeah. So what do you want?"

"Man, they found him with a knife in his chest."

I stared the man down again, unwilling to accept the harsh reality.

"Do you wanna go see him?"

"*Can* I see him?"

"Yeah, man, you just have to go see the police."

The police were the last people who I wanted to see, but if there was any chance for Billy to get a proper burial, for his family to know what happened to him, it was me.

I found a cop and told him that one of my friends had died

and I needed to identify the body. The good news is that there were always cops around the Bowery, so it was easy to get to the morgue.

The morgue, as it turned out, was inside a hospital—kind of a sick joke if you ask me. Hospitals were supposed to be for sick people getting better, not dead people to stay dead.

The cop tapped a nurse on the shoulder and whispered something into her ear. She approached me, and smiled with her mouth, but not her eyes. "You can come with me, dear."

The cop, the nurse, and I walked down hallway after hallway. Finally, we turned into a small, brightly lit room. It looked like a hospital room, but it didn't have hardly anything in it.

"Have a seat and we'll be ready for you soon."

I nodded. I was glad she was being so nice, but it seemed eerie for her to treat me like I was a patient when I was just a grieving hobo.

I took a seat on a small black chair with plastic arms. The cop stood by the door. A normal person might have thought it was uncomfortable, but compared to the cement, it felt like a five-star hotel.

"Mr. Ridley?" The soft voice of the nurse startled me awake. "I'm so sorry, but, we're ready now."

I stared at her. She looked tired. Maybe it was because it was four in the morning. Or maybe she hated death as much as I did. "You can follow me," she said.

I stood up and followed her out of the room, thankful that the night's booze hadn't fully worn off yet. We walked into a neighboring room where a gurney with a white sheet over it was positioned perfectly in the middle of the room. I knew that my friend was under the sheet. I knew that I would have to look.

"I can move the sheet for you, if you want," she said.

"No, I've got it," I replied. Death didn't freak me out. It wasn't scary. It was just unnerving and depressing.

I grabbed the sheet above where the head was and took a short breath in before pulling it back. It was Billy.

His face was pale, and he wasn't smirking the way he usually did. There was a splash of dried blood on his neck, but I couldn't see the wound. His hair seemed a bit more disheveled than usual. I wanted to fix it—give him a little bit of dignity.

"Mr. Ridley?" asked the nurse. "Do you know who this is?"

I looked at Billy again and said, "No ma'am, but I know who he *was*."

Once I had identified him, they were able to get in touch with his next of kin. They thanked me for my time and asked me if there was anyone who could come get me. I asked them to just kindly point me in the direction of the closest, cheapest bar. Ten minutes later, I had a drink in my hand—on the house, thanks to a sympathetic bartender.

In a way, it was probably better that someone killed Billy, instead of some*thing* killing him. That's the only way that the police got involved with anyone who died in the Bowery.

When I saw her, I knew she didn't belong. Her hair was too well kept, and even with the tears in her eyes, her face didn't show the wear of street life like the rest of the women did. I tried to ignore her, but she walked right up to me.

"Are you the renegade?" she asked, hesitantly. "Yes, ma'am, and who are you?" I replied.

"I was with the police. They said you had a red beard; they said you knew him. They said you knew my brother Billy." A tear fell out of her eye, but she didn't bother to brush it away. I didn't know what to say, so I just stood there, staring at her.

"He used to tell me about you," she continued. "He said you

were a good friend and a good brother."

"In a way I feel like it's my fault, what happened to him," she said. "I could have sent him money, I could have found a friend that he could have stayed with, I could have gotten him help or—" Her voice caught, her words hung in the air, silence and sadness filling the space between us.

"Is there anything I can do for you?" I asked.

"Do you want to leave?" she asked.

"Excuse me?"

"Do you want to leave here? I could buy you a plane ticket. My parents know all about it. They said you can stay with us."

I thought for a moment about having a warm bed, a safe house and food on the table every day. It would be any home-less man's dream, but every benefit held one major con. There would be no booze, no freedom, and no release.

"Oh honey..." I said. "I can't do that. You're sweet for offering though." She was beautiful, and that made my refusal even more difficult.

She sniffed a little and nodded. "Okay."

"Is there anything else that I can do?"

"No, no, but please, take this." She placed a folded bill in my hand. "For taking care of my brother."

I looked more closely at her. You could hardly tell that she was Billy's sister. "Well goodbye," she said. "I have to go bury my brother now."

Death was really the worst part of being there. You knew you could die at any moment. That's the thing about existing somewhere in between living and dying. You never know when you're going to push it too far and end up dead. And once you die in the Bowery, that's it. No one remembers you. No one remembers anything about your personality or your hopes or your dreams. No one cries, because no one knows. You just stop existing.

One day, I got up the courage and I asked Pete what they did with the bodies that they took.

"Who do they call?" I asked.

"Usually, nobody." He took a drag of a cigarette and passed it off to me. "They wait until they've got six of them and then they put them all in cardboard coffins and lay them in a mass grave up at Potters Field."

More so than death, I was terrified by this. I was terrified by the idea of meaninglessness and purposelessness, of living for thirty, forty, fifty years with nothing to show for it and no one to remember that I had existed. But at the same time, would I really want anyone to remember me as the drunk that I was?

I wanted to leave right then and there. I wanted to hitchhike back to Milford, run if I had to, just to see if someone would give me another chance, to see if I could make something of myself. But I remembered the look in my father's eyes and the look in Arty's eyes. No one wanted anything to do with me, and they definitely didn't want to take a chance on me. In fact, I probably wasted my only shot by declining Billy's sister's offer. The thought haunted me.

So, my options were: I could choose to stay where I was, learn from the best, and maybe survive long enough to be a hero or at least, have a heroic moment, something worth remembering. I knew that I wasn't stupid. I knew that no one wanted to remember that their son, brother, or friend ended up a worthless drunk. I think that's why everyone was always so proud of Arty. He managed to make something of himself, something worth remembering, which is more than most of the other Ridley kids could say.

What was the point of leaving? It wouldn't put me in any better position. My father wouldn't help me; my brothers wouldn't help me. The only person who seemed willing to help me was Pete. Funny that the people that you're taught not to trust seemed to have been the only ones who cared about me. I decided to stay on with Pete for a while longer.

A couple of months later, I was sitting out on the street when it was starting to get dark. I should have known better than to stay out that late. I was hardly a newcomer at that point, but I was so comfortable, so warm, and so very much enjoying my hard-earned bottle of booze. That's the thing about living on the streets. If you're good at it, it's not so bad during the daytime, but at night—that's when all the crazies came out.

I saw him coming a block away. He walked differently than the rest of the people out at that time of night. I hadn't seen him before, but I had seen that *look* before. He ran right up to me.

"Gimme yer bottle!"

"Get your own! I earned this one." I moved to tuck the bottle under my coat, but as I did, he dove on top of me.

"Give it to me!" His eyes met mine, yellow, pupils wide. He reached for my hand, but I shoved him back. He staggered away and looked at me. A car passed by, its headlights causing a bright reflection on the object in his left hand. It was a knife.

He was still staring at me, so I looked down and saw my own red blood staining my shirt and coat in an expanding circle.

I smashed the bottle, creating a sharp, fragmented weapon. No. That son-of-a-gun was not going to steal my booze and he was definitely not going to steal my life and seal my fate to Potter's Field. I jumped and ran toward him, cursing him loudly.

I chased him down two blocks before we were spotted by two policemen. "Stop!" they yelled. "Stop in the name of the law!"

"This son of a—!" I took a shaky breath in, but didn't stop running. "He stabbed me!" I was about twenty paces away from him when an officer slammed me into the wall of a building.

"We said stop!"

"Didn't you hear me?" I yelled. "He stabbed me! Look!"

The officer cursed and grabbed me by the arm. "Come on, we'll get you to the hospital."

"I can't pay for that," I said. "I know—"

"Get that man!"

"My partner's got it, but you have to get to the hospital now. Do you want to get in my car on your own, or do I have to force you?"

I grunted and allowed the officer to usher me into his car. At the hospital he stayed outside my room for a while. He said something about having to get a statement. I don't know what more they needed to hear. After all, he stabbed me! That much was obvious.

The doctor came in and told me that though there was a lot of blood, the other man hadn't hit any vital organs. With a few stitches, I would be fine. In a way, I had wanted to stay in their nice warm bed overnight, but I also wanted to go get a bottle to replace the one I had broken.

"Officer Dan is going to take you back to where he picked you up. You can come to the clinic and get a clean dressing in two days if you want. You understand?"

I mock saluted. "Clear as day, doc."

By the time I got back, it was nearly light out, so I headed down to the mission to see if they could give me some clothes to replace the blood-stained ones.

And that was that. Near death experience or not, your survival is your own responsibility when you're on the streets. No one else is going to help you. They're too busy trying to survive on their own.

# 6

## 1971

OFF AND ON I considered trying to get sober. It seemed that there were only two ways to get out of the Bowery. Either sober up or die. As much as I hated getting sober, young me was terrified to die.

One night, I checked into a local flophouse called The Comet. I got a cheap room for just over a dollar for the night and I set out determined to sleep off all the alcohol and wake up sober.

"Here," I said to the man at the counter. "Take this bottle of wine and if I look like I'm getting too sick, bring it up to me." I had been through DTs a few times and I knew that it could get ugly. People could die trying to quit cold turkey.

"Sure thing, Renegade." He put the bottle under the counter. I thanked him and headed up to my room to sleep.

I woke up shaking. Sweat coated my body, yet I was so hot I couldn't sleep. I didn't want to sleep. I wanted to puke. I looked beside my bed. It looked like I already had. Ants covered the vomit on the floor. They were moving quickly. They swarmed together and formed terrifying shapes on the walls. Voices filled my head and the figures on the wall began to talk to me.

*I'm going to die.*

I grabbed the hotel phone, but my hands were shaking so badly I couldn't dial the number for the front desk. What was the number for the front desk anyways? Did the phones even work?

I threw myself out of bed and ran out the door and down the four flights of stairs to the lobby area.

The man at the desk saw me. "Renegade? Oh, my..." The next thing I knew he had me in his arms and was pouring the bottle of wine I had given him down my throat. "You're going to be okay, man. Here." He wrapped one of my arms around his shoulder and ushered me back up the steps to my room and back into my bed. By the time we got back the ants had calmed down. There were no dancing figures on my walls. The only thing on the floor was a small pile of vomit. I found myself wondering where they all went, but then I realized they were never there to begin with.

I fell back asleep and when I woke up, I owed another night's stay to the owner. The bottle next to my bed was empty, and a second bottle was half full. I chugged the rest of it and packed my things.

The man at the desk who'd helped me saw me coming again. "You doing all right, buddy? Thought we were gonna lose you yesterday."

"Better now, thanks to you," I said, raising the mostly empty second bottle in his direction.

"Don't mention it. Just promise me one thing. Never ever try to get sober on your own. You're chronic, man. It's just a bad idea."

I nodded. "Thanks again," I said, dropping another two dollars on the counter. He took the money and gave me a sad smile.

"Take care now."

I nodded again. "You too."

I found Panhandle Pete running a scam a few streets down.

"What've you been doing, Renegade? We thought you were a goner!"

"Spent a night at the flophouse. You got room for one more?"

"You know the drill. You get the ones I miss a street down."

We continued living that way for a couple more months. We had a routine. We knew how to play off each other. Of course, not everything we did was a scam. Some of it was just plain begging.

One thing about living in the Bowery is that we were a sort of tourist attraction. People would come down the road on those open top tour buses and just look at us like we were animals in a zoo. We would chase those buses down the street, yelling and hollering. It's degrading, I know, but when you're hopped up on paint thinner, you really don't think twice about it. The people on the buses would pull out their cameras and take pictures while we reached up to catch the rain of nickels and dimes that they threw at us.

It was a predictable way to make a little bit of money, so no one cared how it looked. We would line the streets just waiting for those buses to come by, catch the change, and then watch them leave, going back to their jobs, warm houses, and cookie-cutter lives.

One day Panhandle Pete and I were getting ready to head

out together and I had a burst of courage. "Do you think I could go out on my own?" I asked.

"You could have gone any time you wanted."

"But do you think I'm ready?"

He smiled at me, and playfully gestured down the street. "Go forth, young man!"

I packed a grip with a change of clothes and a bottle of booze and headed out of the city. A few miles outside of the city, there was a train station. Every morning, the trains came in loaded with crops and other supplies from the west. Every evening, they left empty.

I took the subway out late at night. It was better to go late at night because I blended in better. For all the homeless in the Bowery, it was nothing compared to the subways of New York City. While we felt invisible, those living underground *were* invisible. No one saw them curled up next to a heater on a cold winter night. No one saw them almost step out in front of a bus because they were so deliriously drunk, tired, and hungry. They were nothing in anybody's eyes, not even a sad sight, a nuisance or an eyesore.

The subway sped out of the city and finally emerged above ground. As we cruised through the suburbs, lights clicked off in the houses as we passed them, people settling in for the night. I imagined them safe and warm with their families. I tried to remember the last night I had spent with my family. It must have been some time before I got arrested and sent to the Army. It was funny to think that back then, I didn't know I was having my last night that could be considered anything close to normal.

Uncomfortable with the thoughts that I was thinking, I pulled out one of my two wine bottles, concealed in a paper bag, and took a few swigs, letting the alcohol displace the sadness.

It was a short walk to the station from the end of the commuter train. On my way to the station, I passed some other men. One was in a suit. One looked like he was coming home from college or something. Most of the others were like me, wearing hand-me down jackets that were buttoned up under long, unkempt beards, and holding small bags.

We knew better than to stand close together. Everyone was always more suspicious of a group of hobos than they were any one individual. And besides that, I'm sure most train companies anticipated one hobo would hop their train. I'm also sure that they wouldn't be okay with ten of us boarding at the same time.

There must have been at least 100 cars, ranging from new and clean to coal-covered and graffiti-tagged. All I knew about the train was that it was going to go west, but anything would be better than dying here and heading straight to Potter's Field. I found a car about a third of the way from the back, a forgettable grey boxcar tagged with peeling blue paint. I pulled myself up and checked to make sure I was alone.

Feeling certain that I was, I shut the door and felt my way to the back corner where, even if someone did open the door, it would be hard to see me. I curled up in a ball in the corner, closed my eyes, and waited to see where the train would take me.

# 7

## 1971

THE TRAIN CONSTANTLY SEEMED to change speed at night. Slowing down as it went into a curve or up a mountain, speeding up as it coasted back down. I slept, but not well, until finally the sharp squeal of rusting wheels woke me up for good. The train was slowing, slowing, slowing until finally it stopped. I waited, half expecting a police officer to throw open the door and drag me out. But nothing happened.

What time was it? Some light shined in through cracks around the closed door. Morning? Noon? It was hard to tell. I was always a good sleeper and, especially after a night of drinking, I had been known to sleep all day.

I grabbed my bottle of wine and took a long drink before I stood up.

Cautiously, I picked up my pack and went to the door. Here

I went, stepping out into my new life, with no turning back now.

I pushed the door, and thankfully, no one had locked it from the outside. I was near the end of the train, so I could see the station that the locomotive had pulled into. It was a modest size, and in the distance sprawled a sea of homes that turned into businesses and then finally high rises. It was hard to tell where I was. Chicago? Maybe. It didn't matter. Anywhere but skid row sounded good to me.

I hopped off the boxcar, my body was rattling as I hit the ground. Aches suddenly appeared in my arms, neck, back and legs. I thought for sure that I was going to fall over from the pain, but surprisingly, I stayed upright. I took a few cautious steps forward before deciding it was going to take more than a sip of wine to get me through this day. I grabbed at my bottle again and realized there were only a few sips left in the first bottle. *I knew I should have packed more.*

Opposite the city, a few hundred yards away, there was a thin forest. Looking around for people, I hopped off the boxcar and jogged over the edge of the forest. The sun was warm, but the breeze was cool on my face. Judging by where the sun was, I figured it was early morning, meaning that the night was going to be cold but bearable. I had certainly slept in worse.

I found a bush that looked well-protected from the wind and stashed my gear inside of it. I knew that I could crash there for a day, but it wasn't going to be enough long term. I made a small fire and began making a mental list of all the things I needed to do to survive on the road. First was alcohol. The stuff I brought with me wouldn't last very long. Second was food. Clothing. Protection. Heat. Definitely heat. Even sitting there in the shade, I realized that it wasn't quite warm enough to sleep comfortably outside. Checking to make sure my pack was secure, I splashed some water on my face from a nearby creek and headed toward the trainyard to see what I could find.

As it turned out, exploring the trainyard and the homes around it wasn't that much different than exploring the streets of New York City. The more you looked like you knew what you were doing, the less likely people were to think you didn't belong there.

The surrounding neighborhood was nice, but residential. Empty trash cans littered the road and fancy cars passed by me every couple of minutes.

Though I was able to find a few things that would help keep me warm and protect me if need be, that was probably the worst part about leaving New York City and Panhandle Pete and all the other guys I knew. There was no hope of protection. Sure, I had heard of hobo colonies and camps, but I doubted I would find one on my first night. Just to be safe, I grabbed a few shards of glass and tucked them into my coat pockets and headed back to my camp for the night. Tomorrow was a new day, and I could always move closer to the city.

When I got back, my coals had gone out and the sun was starting to go down. I grabbed my bottle, ready to finish it off when I heard laughter in the distance. It sounded like there were two or three men. I smelled smoke, but it was from fresh wood, not the dying embers of my fire. The noise scared me so much I tripped over my sack and crashed into the trees.

"Hey! Someone's out here!" I heard someone call. "Another tramp? No way," someone else said.

I heard the rustling of a man walking through the trees and bushes. I quickly shoved my wine under my bed roll and wrapped my hand loosely around the glass in my coat. I could feel my pulse rising as I planned my exit in case things turned ugly. Finally, a body emerged from the foliage.

"Hey! You been here long?" called a man with a short greying beard. Definitely not a cop or a railway worker. You could tell by the way he was dressed.

"Who's asking?" I said. I had learned a long time ago not to answer any questions first. It was all about learning how to get the information you needed while revealing as little as possible about yourself.

"You can call me Chip. You're set up not far from my camp. You need a place to stay?"

"I have a little camp," I said, "but I'd be happy to join you for supper."

"You have anything?" he asked.

"A bit of bread," I said, leaving out the wine.

"Broth, bread and beer. Sounds like a good meal to me. This way."

Chip was so confident I just followed him without thinking too deeply about it. Still, I kept the glass in my left hand. He led me through the brush to a little clearing with a low burning fire in the center. Chip had built a roof between two trees and had his bed roll laid out underneath it. Around the fire were two other hobos, bundled up in oversized coats.

"We've got another one!" Chip said to the two men. "What do they call you?"

"Renegade," I said.

"Renegade!" Chip laughed. "I like that! Renegade, this is Pops and Jack. Sit down and I'll get you a bowl. You can set your bread over here."

I had hardly set the bread down before the two men each ripped off a sizable hunk and started dipping it in the broth. The smell of onions and potatoes hit my nostrils and suddenly

I realized I hadn't eaten in over a day.

"So, Renegade," Pops asked, crumbs sprinkling from his mouth to his unkempt beard, "how long've you been out here?"

"Just today," I said. Chip handed me a bowl of soup and I thanked him.

"Well of course, you just got here today. I mean how long have you been riding trains?"

"Not very long," I said, wondering how my being a new-comer would go over amongst this crowd. "A few weeks."

"Weeks?" Jack looked up from his bread just long enough to look me in the eyes.

"Maybe a few months," I backtracked. "It's hard to keep track."

"It don't matter how long he's been out here," Chip said. "Just so long as he follows the rules and don't bring no bulls our way." Chip looked back at me. "The city's a good one. Lotsa people willing to give an old hobo a couple-a coins. Plus, the rail yard is so big they can't keep track of every car there, so whenever yer ready to leave, you shouldn't have much of a problem."

"Sounds good," I said. "You know where a fella can get some more booze around here?"

"There's a couple-a good places down in town. I can show you around tomorrow if you want."

"Thank you." We ate in silence for a little bit. The warm soup and fire helped fight off the chill of the evening.

"You want some of your bread, Renegade?" Jack asked.

I reached out my hand and Jack got a worried look on his face. "You okay?"

I looked down to see a cut across my hand, shallow, but bloody from my grip on the glass.

"Oh, yes, I must have just fallen on a rock or something

when Chip showed up. It was sure a surprise!"

"Okay," Jack said cautiously. "You gotta be more careful out here. No hospital's gonna take you in unless you're dying."

"He's got that right," added Pops. "I had a friend lost his whole hand. By the time he got to the hospital, they just cut it off, stitched it up and sent him back out to camp. Whole thing took less than a day."

"Oh, I heard about him," said Chip. "Then the hospital had the nerve to send the police out to try and get some kinda payment."

"He woulda got away too," added Jack, "if he would've jumped the train instead of sittin' in it."

"What's wrong with sitting?" I asked.

"The bulls'll come and check the cars at night. If you've been sittin' you need to start hoppin'. Otherwise you're just a sittin' duck," said Jack.

"Yup. You wait till the train's gettin' started, then run and pull yourself up," said Pops.

"Takes a try or two to get it right, but it's way better. Plus, once you're on the train, they can't stop you," said Jack, picking at his teeth. "The most they can do is stop the train, and then you just hop off and disappear 'fore the train has a chance to stop at the station."

I nodded.

"Hey brother, you'll be fine. Just always make sure you have something to offer and you'll always have a friend out here," said Chip. "We hobos have to take care of each other."

"Yeah, man, cause nobody else sure did," Pops said.

"That's for sure," we all agreed.

The next morning Chip showed me the fastest way into the city, showed me the best places for some wine, at my request, and showed me where he usually set up in the morning.

"You can make enough to live on here," he said. "But don't take my business." He smiled when he said the words, but a dullness in his eyes said that he meant every word.

The first couple of weeks were hard. I only stayed in Chicago for a few days before moving on to the next city. I stayed just long enough to get money for two bottles of wine and then I'd move on out. Wine you had to buy (usually). But food could come from anywhere. I learned when the restaurants would get rid of the food that they couldn't sell. I would snatch it out of the trash bin before the flies and rats got to it. The Christian organizations would help too. They gave out food and clothing to help out with our basic needs, but they never included alcohol. And if you were in as poor of luck as the guys I knew, alcohol was just as great a need as water.

The next couple of months were easier. By that time, I had been a full-fledged hobo for a year; I was one of the best. It wasn't much different from when I went to live in New York City. I had to find where I could get some free clothes and food, and where I could sleep if the weather got too cold. I had to learn the right places to beg and the kind of scams that worked on the people of that particular town. In fact, I felt *too* good at it, at times. Where was the challenge? Where was the excitement?

I was restless. I couldn't bear to stay in the same place too long. So, every couple of weeks, I'd pack my bag, say goodbye to the men I'd been camping with, and find the next train out. The northern rails were the best to ride in the summer, and the southern rails in the winter. Sure, the winter rails were a bit crowded, but it was worth it to know that you would be warm and safe rather than freezing to death in a barn somewhere.

The best part about riding the rails was making camp and

meeting the other train riders, hobos, tramps, whatever you call them. I had a bit of a reputation among the other hobos. I wanted them to know that if you came to Floyd's camp, you'd find a cigarette, some booze, and a bowl of beans. Over the years that I ran the rails, I must have started hundreds of camps.

# 8

## FALL 1975

BEING DRUNK ALL THE TIME took a toll on my body, whether it was from the alcohol or from the reckless things that I tended to do. One day, I jumped off a freight train in Lincoln, Nebraska and broke my ankle. The bone nearly popped out and everything. I don't remember exactly who found me, but the pain was so blinding, I didn't care. They took me to the hospital and I had to stay there for a number of days.

Most of those hospital workers had never met a hobo, and they definitely had never gotten to know one after nights and nights and nights in a hospital. Of course, I didn't have any insurance, so I kept asking when I could leave and if I had to pay. The nice nurses would assure me that everything was taken care of and that they knew I couldn't pay, but the less nice nurses would barely talk to me.

One nurse in particular caught my eye. Her name was Wanda Kay. She had a soft, sweet smile, long dark hair and she was constantly stopping by to see how I was doing.

I told her about my mother and father, how they both were no good drunks and how I had inherited everything straight from them. I told her how no one wanted to help me, so I just did the only thing I knew to do. And the more I talked and told her my story, the more she kept coming back to hear more.

"They're going to release you today, Floyd," she said.

"That so?" I asked.

"Yes." She hesitated and smoothed her uniform. "I thought that since we were having such a nice time getting to know each other that you might like to keep in touch."

"That sounds very nice," I said in my most handsome voice.

She smiled a full, bright smile. "Here's my telephone number and my address." She handed me a slip of paper. "You can call any time."

I sat in bed and stared at her as she stood next to me and looked into my eyes.

"Is there anything else?" I asked.

"No, no!" She said, almost startled. "I just…I hope this won't be the last time we talk."

I assured her that it wouldn't be and we parted ways. An hour or so later another nurse came to teach me how to use crutches and then usher me to the exit.

At this point, I had been sober for a while—as sober as you can be while on pain medication. I hadn't had a drink in over a week. Any time I found myself sober I always wondered if I could make it stick.

It was a process, for sure. Every once in a while, I would check myself into a facility, just if I was getting too out of hand with the drinking or if I felt like my body needed a break. They would help me get sober. I'd get out, hop the next train out of that city and be drunk again less than a day later.

Was I incapable of quitting? Was it just so chronic that I had no choice in the matter?

I didn't know, but on this day, I wanted to stay sober, at least long enough so that I could go see Wanda Kay again.

A nice policeman offered me a place to stay with him and his wife, and I looked into a job at a local construction site. It was hard work, but I didn't mind it. Wanda Kay and I met up a few times, but the thought of drinking began to consume my mind again.

I knew that she wouldn't want me drinking, and the policeman I was living with sure didn't want me drinking, so I left town. I went straight to skid row in Sioux City, Iowa. I hadn't saved very much from my construction job, and Wanda Kay seemed to really like me, so I got a few coins together and called her on a payphone.

"Wanda?"

"Floyd Ridley! What are you doing? Where are you? Are you OK?"

"Of course, I'm okay Wanda. I just wanted to see if you could send me some money. You see, I really just need a little to get me on my feet; I'm in Sioux City, Iowa, you can—"

"Stay put, I'll be right there."

"Wanda, you don't have to—"

"I said stay put, you fool!"

With that she hung up. She hopped in her car almost right away and drove out to pick me up. Her face showed lines of worry. "You can't just run off like that!" she scolded. "We had no idea what happened to you!"

"I was fine, Wanda."

"Fine? You call sleeping on the street, calling me up for money *fine?*" Women. They never understood.

She took me straight to her apartment, but I was so addicted I couldn't stop drinking. "It's this city," she decided, throwing her hands in the air. "It has to be this city. It's not fair for you to be here."

"Where else can we go, sweetheart?" I asked.

"I hear Arizona's nice," she said. "We could get married and maybe find some work together..." her voice trailed off. "No, I'm sorry if I sound foolish."

"You're not foolish, Wanda. You're a college-educated woman! If you say Arizona is the place to be, then I believe you."

She smiled and kissed me on the cheek. "I'll make some calls."

Not long after that day we packed all our belongings into a truck and moved out to Arizona. Wanda Kay had found an apartment complex that we could manage together, and when we arrived, she found a priest to marry us. Within a few months, she was pregnant.

And I was constantly drunk. Now, Wanda had been tolerant of my drinking up until that point, but it was like a switch was flipped and my kind, understanding, motherly wife became someone I barely knew.

We named our baby Jennifer. By the time she was born, I was losing jobs left and right. I would stay out late and go in late for work. Eventually, I just stopped showing up and spent whole days at the bar, laughing with the bartender, and making friends with whoever came my way.

Wanda Kay was as patient as she could be for about seven months and then she simply wasn't patient anymore. I had come home just after midnight and I waltzed into our bedroom like I was the king of England.

"Hi, Baby Girl!" I said, picking up Jennifer out of her bassinet. I kissed my daughter and looked up at Wanda Kay. "Hey, beautiful."

Wanda Kay looked at me. She looked through me. She was processing something in her mind. "You're drunk again."

"Wanda, baby…"

"For goodness sake Floyd! We have a baby! Either you get sober, or you get out of here." Her voice shook, but her eyes showed that she meant it. Every prior empty threat meant nothing. She was serious.

"It's…it's not that easy, baby. Come on, you know I'm trying."

"Oh, so, while you were trying not to drink you decided to go to a bar? Yeah right."

"It's not easy for me either, baby. But I'll do better. I love you…"

Tears poured down her face. "No," she said. "No. You don't. And I don't even care if you do. I can't take care of you anymore. Jennifer needs me." She motioned for me to give our baby to her.

It was like passing my life away. Sure, I was drunk, but my feelings for her and that baby were just as real and deep as before. I kissed Jennifer on the head and passed her to her mother, the one who was going to raise her.

"No more chances, Floyd," she said. She closed her eyes. "Now get out."

"Baby…"

"Out. Now."

I quickly packed a few of my things and left, shutting the door on her muffled sobs.

Looking back, I could have stuck around and checked into a facility. I could have really tried to get sober. But, instead, I found the closest train and hopped on, determined to put miles and miles and miles between me and that sweet baby and her mama. I wanted to make them a faint memory, something that I could wonder whether it had been real or just a very bad dream. But every mile only deepened the hurt in both of our hearts.

Now, don't think I was a deadbeat dad. I had wanted to be a dad so badly. If I had known how to be a dad, I would have done it in an instant. But I think a part of me thought that it was better for her anyways. I mean look at me. I grew up with a drunk for a father and what happened to me? Nothing good.

When I would ride the northern rails, I would always stop and look for Jenny and her mama. Years went by and finally a priest told me that she had changed her name and moved away. No one in the town had even really heard from her recently, let alone left a message for me or left any way for me to find her. Upon hearing this news, I did what I always did. I hopped another train.

# 9

SOON AFTER WE SPLIT UP, I left for California. There was a thriving hobo community out there. Besides, it was warm and there were plenty of places to hustle, drink, and sleep.

I was in California when the "Slasher" was on the loose. Even though I usually ran alone, I partnered up with a guy named Billy. He had read about the Slasher in one of the papers and I had heard about him from a couple of the hobos that I knew.

Nobody was safe. We were never really safe, but by the time you have been on the road a few years, you can start to have a false sense of security. You can start to feel like you have it all figured out. But just like that guy in New York who stabbed me, you can never really see what's coming.

The Slasher would stab homeless men and cut their throats. The police later said that he left cups of blood around the men, along with other satanic items. You get used to being a little scared on the streets, so when you read something like this, you know you have to do something.

So, Billy and I buddied up for a while. We would take turns sleeping at night while the other one kept watch. We did our best to stay even more hidden than usual, sticking to the bush, moving our camp around so the Slasher wouldn't know where we were staying. By the time he was caught, he had killed eleven hobos and was trying to kill another one.

I never found out why he did it. I guess nobody did. That's for him and God to sort out whenever God and him should meet.

Maybe we were all just easy targets. If you were going to cause someone a tough time, it made sense to pick an under-nourished, yellow-skinned hoboinstead of a fit businessman or someone who would out-fight you or be reported missing right away.

I remember a time in Riverside when I was with my partner in a bar and got surrounded by a bunch of Hell's Angels. My buddy and I were hanging out in a bar late at night, spending the day's earnings on cheap beer and swindling the good stuff from other bar-goers when we could.

"Look over there," my buddy said. "Actually, don't look. Just trust me; it's trouble."

Casually, I looked over my shoulder and saw two men in their signature black jackets standing by the door.

"S***," I said.

"Be cool. It's a free country. They can drink here if they want."

I appreciated my friend's optimism, but we both knew that they were looking for me. What could I say, I didn't know the girl I liked was with the Angels! (Honestly, though, I don't think it would have made a difference.)

We drank for another hour or so as two, four, five more men joined the posse sitting by the door.

I motioned to the bartender. "Hey, mind if I sneak out the back? Those guys have my number and I gotta get home to my wife and kid." I knew he'd be more sympathetic if he thought I had someone to go home to. He agreed and nodded toward the door.

"Go quick. I don't want any fightin' in here tonight."

"Yes sir," I said, paying him the last of my bill for the night.

My friend leaned over. "You need me to come with you?"

"Nah, wait here and follow after me in about twenty minutes. No reason for you to risk life and limb too."

The alcohol in my body made me push past fear and walk out with my head held high.

*Whack!*

Something hit me hard, out of the blue, behind my knees. I felt my legs give out and rocks dig into the skin on my legs as I fell forward on the asphalt.

"Can't hide from us, Renegade," said an unidentifiable voice. Another blow landed on me, this time on my side, throwing me to the ground.

"You thought our girl wouldn't tell us you were trying to get to her?" Someone kicked me in the stomach and I rolled onto my back. I looked up just in time to see a two-by-four headed straight for my chest.

*Crack!* I went blind immediately from the pain. Was the sound I heard the board breaking or something inside of me? I curled into a ball to protect myself.

"Don't worry, Renegade," said the voice. "This is the last time you'll have to worry about her...or us. When we're done with you, you won't have to worry about anything."

The group laughed together like a group of hyenas and the blows kept coming on every side.

"Guys!" Was that the bartender? "Drinks on the house. Get your sorry a\*\*es back in here."

I heard the Angels grumble among themselves before their footsteps faded off into the night. I heard the door shut. I wanted to move and run away, but even alcohol couldn't fix the way I was feeling. I opened my eyes and tried to look for obvious injuries, but I couldn't see much in the dim light.

Someone ran toward me. "Floyd?" It was my friend. "What did they do to you? Can you get up?"

"I don't want to get up."

"Come on, we don't have much time." My buddy tried to grab my right arm and I yelped in pain.

"Other arm, other arm," I instructed. He walked me to a nearby hospital and dropped me off at the emergency department. I didn't blame him for not staying; that's just not the way things work on the street.

I tried to explain to the hospital workers that I couldn't pay and they should just let me leave, but they said that they had to help since I looked like death itself. After an x-ray and a bunch of tests, they decided I had a broken collar bone and put me in a sling for six weeks.

I hated being injured more than anything. There was nothing worse than being on the streets and being unable to bring in any money or protect myself. I gathered what I needed to stay drunk for a few weeks and hid in a bush outside the city.

At least, this wasn't as bad as a few weeks earlier when I'd been shot in a turf war; so thankfully, I knew what to do. That time, I didn't go to a hospital at all. You usually don't go when you live on the street because it can get you in more trouble than just taking care of your injury on your own.

The bullet was lodged by my rib cage. By the time I had gotten back to my bush, I had blood all down my shirt and pants. I took my fingers and touched the wound. Fire like pain shot through my body. I rolled up a rag and put it in my mouth to bite on and tried again. This time I got my fingers inside the hole. I could feel the round, slippery bullet wedged by two of my ribs. I wrapped my fingers around it and pulled it out quickly.

Now that the bullet was out, I knew I needed to close the wound, so I made a mud patty and put it on top, then wrapped some cloth around my chest. I stayed in the bush for six weeks that time too, drinking what I had and changing out my mud bandage every day.

After the Angels beat me up, I decided I ought to head back to Arizona, where it was warm and much safer than LA. The bars were just as good.

When I was drinking in a bar, I was in my element. Much like my mother, I had a likeable personality. Sure, those who knew me personally didn't seem to care about me, but give me ten minutes and a couple of shots of whiskey and I could make myself into the most well-loved son-of-a-gun in the whole town.

I used my charm, my personality, but I gave myself a totally different life story. There's something about pretending to be a guy who had his life much more together than I did that gave me a good feeling. It was like I got to live out somebody else's life, if only for a few hours.

"Back in 'Nam," I'd say, getting ready to spin a story.

"You're a vet? Here, allow me," someone would say, motioning the bartender over with a five-dollar bill. "Get him whatever he wants!"

Everyone knew the Vietnam vets got the worst deal when

they came back. So many people were against the war; it wasn't an odd thing to come across a vet down on his luck, forgotten by his former friends and coworkers.

I took on all sorts of personalities. War veteran, local surgeon, you name it. Somewhere out there, I can promise you that there are still men talking about the time they met a war veteran doctor in a bar and talked all night. There's a whole group of guys that remember meeting someone who didn't exist.

Getting free drinks in a bar was all part of the gig. I'd been sober enough times to know that if the booze stopped running, so would I. There was nothing more terrifying than waking up without a bottle to pick me up. Without it, I was practically mute, fully-terrified. Embarrassed. And no hustle works if you're not completely confident. I needed it. I needed the alcohol to draw out that boisterous, confident man that seemed to live inside me.

So, I kept moving. The most dangerous thing for a hobo running a scam is getting caught. Not only does that mean you can't make any more money, but it means you're just minutes away from being chased out of town by the police. You can tell when you're starting to push your luck, staying in a place too long. The bartender starts looking at you funny, someone mentions that your story sounds familiar. It's time to get out.

One time, the cops caught up with me and I had to run out of town fast. I had little regard for the law anymore. I don't mean that I would steal or anything, but I would do everything I could to stay far away from police officers. I didn't mind being homeless, but I knew that I wouldn't survive a second round in prison. The moment people started asking questions or the cops started hanging around too much, I was out of there.

Normally, I would try to find a nice open car, but in a

pinch, you had to be open to different options. I ran over to a bridge that I knew crossed over the railroad tracks and waited. In the distance, I could see the lights coming from the front car, shining bright light onto the tracks in front of it. I ducked down and waited until the engine passed under me, shaking the bridge and piercing my ears with its deafening horn. Then I stood up and looked down. Coal cars. It was a best-case scenario, believe it or not.

I stood up on the edge of the bridge. One jump would either save me or kill me. It was frightening, but more so, it was exhilarating.

*One...*

It wasn't a long jump. I readied myself to launch into the coal cars.

*Two...*

Each heartbeat shook my entire chest.

*Three...*

What would it matter if I missed anyways?

*Jump.*

I must have closed my eyes, because I felt the coal before I saw it. Coarse rocks scraped my legs as I sunk in, chest deep. Coal dust blew up and into my face. I turned away and tried to shield my face, but it was impossible. I pushed through the coal to a corner of the car and held on, turning my face so that I could breathe. I looked back at the city, its lights getting dimmer and dimmer. I breathed a sigh of relief and closed my eyes to try to sleep.

When the train finally stopped, I dragged myself out of the car and down by the river. My hands were so dirty and coal-covered. Even the soap that I'd gotten from the local mission couldn't wash it off. My skin stayed black for weeks.

Most of the time, I liked to ride alone. It was easier that way. You didn't have to take care of anybody else or worry about them doing something that would ruin your hustle. But from time to time, people would hang out at my hobo camp and we would get to be friends.

It was much different than when I lived in New York City. The guys were much more friendly, more relaxed. Some of them were guys like me, guys who were abandoned by their families and their friends. Guys who figured that they could get more out of life by riding the rails than they could by waiting on a street corner to die.

But some of them were of an entirely different breed. I met men who had been out there since just after the Depression, when train hopping and the hobo lifestyle was brand new. These guys barely drank. Many of them smoked, but mostly, they worked. They were apple pickers in the north during the summer and fall, and orange pickers in the summer. Some of them would work on the loading docks, making just enough money to get some food and new clothes, and maybe stay in a hotel a night or two.

I never really enjoyed working. It was oftentimes much easier just to work a hustle on the street whenever I needed some cash, but I put in some honest work from time to time. Usually, I would work when I felt like my body needed a break from the drinking. In Lincoln, Nebraska, I got a room at the YMCA while I worked unloading trucks, just to get some exercise and keep myself occupied so I couldn't drink so much.

That's where I met a lot of those men. They'd do anything they had to do to make money. When the jobs dried up, they'd move on to a new site. Some of these men were family men, guys who had wives and kids back home, and they were sending them the money they made. Some of them were ex-doctors and ex-lawyers, people who just got tired of living life the way they were told that they should and left everything overnight.

They said that they wanted to live the carefree life. Everything felt meaningless so they were stepping out, hoping to find some meaning. They said that they were finally free.

I never told them, but they weren't really free. They were as free as I was, and I knew I wasn't free. We weren't shackled to our jobs or our desks or our families, but we were shackled to our lifestyles. I didn't know many guys who decided that they wanted to get out and were actually successful.

But we found our own sort of community, even if it was only temporary. We weren't close, but we looked out for one another.

# *10*

ONE TIME, I was running a camp near a bridge in Omaha, Nebraska when I met a man named Jack. Bridges were great. They provided shelter from the wind and the rain, the sun when it was glaring down, but they couldn't protect you from everything.

"You okay, Jack?" I asked.

"Yeah." He coughed and spat something into the ground in front of him. "You okay, Renegade?"

"I'm serious, man," I said feeling his head. "You're burning up."

"Really?" He closed his eyes. "Feels like it's so cold it could be snowing."

"Let me help you, man. The mission has that recovery program. If nothing else, they can get you healthy, okay?"

After some arguing, he agreed, and I checked him into the program. Two weeks later I went down to the mission to get a hot meal for supper and Jack was on the other side of the line serving the mashed potatoes.

"Jack, you look great!" I said, handing my plate to him.

"I feel great," he said. "I'd feel better if I could have a drink though."

"No way, man. You look amazing. You have to stay with it!" The line pressed me forward, so I grabbed my plate with its steaming pile of mashed potatoes. "I'll see you soon!"

A few days later, I had made enough money to spend a night at the bar, so I stopped into a favorite pub of mine.

"Renegade!" the bartender called.

"What's happening?" I called back.

"I gotta talk to you," he said, his voice softening.

"Not before you get me a shot of brandy, huh?" I joked.

"I'm serious, Floyd." He pulled out a newspaper. "Your friend Jack is in here today." He opened the newspaper to the second page and I read the headline. HOMELESS MAN DIES IN ABANDONED BUILDING.

I motioned for some of the other guys to come over and we read the article together. The newspaper said that he had fallen off a beam and broken his back. Death was instantaneous.

We all stared at the article for a while. Even though we only knew each other a few weeks, we were all the closest thing to family anybody had.

"Wait, look here," I said, pointing at a full wine bottle at the bottom of the body bag, just laying there. "What do you think?"

No one said anything for a moment.

"I think God loved him so much," I said. "He took him before he had a chance to drink again. Jack died sober."

That was more than I knew most of us were going to be able to say.

"Renegade, where did you get thoughts like that?"

I didn't know. I certainly didn't believe in God, or like Him very much. But it seemed appropriate. It seemed right. And if God did do Jack that mercy, I wanted to do him one more.

I talked to the pastor at the mission and he helped all of us hobos raise the money to bury him properly. For a hobo, that, in itself, was a major source of dignity. On the day he was buried, five of us were there, representing family and friends alike. Saying goodbye and hoping God would be half as kind to us as He had been to Jack.

It was a few months later that I was living in Denver, drinking with another hobo, when I started vomiting a lot of blood. I had vomited blood before, but this time it wouldn't stop.

"You have to get some help," my buddy said.

"Where? No hospital is going to take me in without insurance."

"I know a detox center a couple of miles north of Denver. You don't need money to go there. We just need to hop a train."

With my buddy's help, we arrived at Greeley, Colorado the next day via freight train. I hadn't seen myself in a mirror for such a long time that I did a double take when I walked by a decorative mirror.

I looked like a ninety-year-old man. I had lost all my teeth and my skin was turning yellow from jaundice. My sunken cheeks were hidden by my buckle-length grey beard, but I could tell I would hardly tip the scale at 110 pounds.

I heard a female voice. "My God, look at this guy." And then, "Mr. Ridley?"

I shook hands with my buddy and followed them back to an

intake room. They stripped the rags I was wearing off me and held me up in the shower so they could scrub me down. They put me in a set of blue pajamas and slippers before leading me to a room with a bed.

When I lay down on that bed, my body sank into the cushions of the mattress. It was softer and more welcoming than any bed I had ever been in.

Not that I had much to compare it with. I had last been in a nice bed when I was married. Quickly, I felt my muscles relaxing and I fell into a deep sleep.

When I woke up, I was shaking. I called out for help, looking around, waiting for the hallucinations to start, preparing my mind to stand strong against the fear they would bring.

"Mr. Ridley, calm down now, you're okay." The nurse said. A doctor came in and gave me medicine to help stop the DTs. When I stopped shaking, they gave me more medicine to help me eat and get my weight up.

At the end of five days, the doctor came in to have a talk with me. "Floyd, we normally only let people stay here in our detox center for five days, but we can't stop the bleeding. You've ruptured all the veins in your esophagus from whatever it is you've been eating and drinking, and the fact is that it's just going to take more time."

I had prepared myself for the news, whether good or bad. I loved my new bed, but I would be fine if they made me leave.

"But frankly, I don't think I could live with myself if you left now. So were going to make an exception."

He went on to explain that they had a lot more work to do, they were going to let me stay in the halfway house in the upstairs of the facility, just until they had fixed everything they could.

"Okay," I said. "Let's go on upstairs!"

One day, I was walking down the stairs from the halfway house and I walked by the office where their secretary worked. Now, when alcoholics sober up, their bodies and their minds wake up. They start noticing things that they wouldn't normally notice, and one of the first things I noticed was Cathy.

She was beautiful—an absolutely incredible looking woman. So, I started making excuses to go see her. I stopped outside her office and said, "Hello, ma'am! How do you like my shoes?" I said, pointing to my blue slippers.

She paused, mouth agape, not sure how to answer.

"I call them my detox rebox," I said with a wink. She laughed and that was the beginning of our relationship.

Finally, about two months later, my esophagus had healed enough for me to leave and they were ready to release me. So, I headed down the stairs to break the bad news to Cathy.

"Hey there, Cathy," I called.

"Hey, Floyd!" she said sweetly, putting down her pen and pushing away her work to give me a hug. "What brings you down here?"

"I came to tell you something," I said, motioning for her to sit down in one of her two office chairs. I sat in the other. "They're letting me go. I'm not going to be able to stay here anymore."

"Where are you going to go?" she asked.

"Probably back on the streets, sweetie," I said. "But don't you worry about me."

"The streets? You'll die!"

I shrugged. "I don't have a choice."

"Yes, you do," she said. She bit her lip as if deciding if she really wanted to say what she was about to say. "You can stay with me. At my house." Nurses always did have compassionate hearts.

"I can't stay with you."

"Cathy?" A doctor poked his head in from the hallway. "A word?"

"One second," she said. She put her soft hands on mine. "I love you. We can do this. You can get a job, and I'll take care of you until you do." Her voice was soft, hovering just above a whisper. She moved one hand to my face and caressed my jaw. "I'll take care of you."

"Cathy!" The doctor called again, louder and more intensely.

"I said one second!" She turned back toward me. "What do you say?"

"You'd better go see what he wants."

"I will, but first promise me you'll move in with me." She looked deep into my eyes. "Promise me."

"I promise," I said. A bed would be nice, I told myself. And she was so very much fun to be with. Maybe this time…

"Great!" She kissed me on the lips. "Wait for me at the bus stop if you get out before I do. I'll take you home."

"Cathy!"

"I'm coming!" she squeezed my hand one more time before leaving. I went back up to my room and got my few belongings together.

As it turned out, her parents didn't want her bringing home a drunk, so she put me up in a hotel for a few days, until she could get her own place.

She lost her job at the detox center for fraternizing with me—I guess it was against the rules to become friends with a patient—but soon got a job as an orderly in a nursing home. We moved into a little apartment together and I tried to find a job too.

I was sober for a few days, but now that I was healthy enough to drink and free from the rules of the detox center, the urge to drink just got stronger and stronger. I would work long enough to get paid, buy booze, and then fail to show up for work again and lose the job. I did what alcohol told me to do.

One night, Cathy was upset with me and said, "I think you should go to Northern Nebraska. They have a really good treatment center there. I think it could help, and my parents have already agreed to pay for it. They have a car ready, if you're willing to go."

I loved her. I loved the way she made me feel. I loved the apartment we had with the safe warm bed. "I'll go, sweetheart."

The program lasted for two weeks, and I managed to stay sober throughout it. When I got home, Cathy's dad was waiting for me.

"I know you two..." he hesitated, "love each other. But if you're going to live together, you need to get married."

Cathy nodded and then looked at me. "What do you say?"

I smiled. "Sounds like a great idea," I said.

We were married the following weekend in her dad's church and got pregnant seven months later. Now, things weren't perfect before she got pregnant, but just like with my previous wife, the baby seemed to change everything.

"I'm not going to bring this child into this world with alcohol in the house and an alcoholic father." It was like I was reliving the past, except this time, I wouldn't even be able to say goodbye to my child. "I'm serious, Floyd. Get straight or I'm gone."

I didn't think she would really leave me. After all, she loved me. She'd ruined her relationship with her parents for me and lost a job for me. She was strong for me, and she knew that without her, I would have no reason to get sober at all. So, I did exactly what I did every night and got roaring drunk. One night, when I got home, there was a note on the table.

*You'll hear from my attorney.*

She was gone. Her clothes were gone. The baby things we had been buying were gone. The pictures of her family that had stood on our bedside table were gone. I felt lucky that I was drunk. If it hurt that much drunk, it would have hurt a million times more if I had been sober.

I packed my own bag and threw on an extra coat. If she wanted me gone, then gone I would be. I grabbed the booze from the kitchen, jumped a freight train and was gone.

Alcohol took all of my emotions. I didn't feel anything. Even when I found out that she had a boy and named him Christopher, I didn't cry. I didn't yell. I felt just as numb as I always had, but still, something in me wanted to call her.

Finally, a few months later, I found a pay phone in southern California. I had the operator find her number and patch me through.

"Are you sober?" were some of the first words out of her mouth.

"Yes."

I lied. I know. Shame on me, but I thought it would be easier on her. She let out a small cry. "I miss you, Floyd. Can I come see you?"

I could tell by her voice that she still loved me. I told her that she could come see me in Riverside. So, she flew out and met me by the airport. As soon as she saw me, she started crying.

"You lied to me," she said touching her finger where her wedding ring used to be. "You're drunk right now, aren't you?"

"I just missed you too. Where's Christopher?" I asked,

evading her question.

"With my parents," she said, composing herself. "Did you ever intend to really get your life straight?"

"I really intended to," I said, telling the truth. I wanted to hold her and kiss her again.

She sighed. "Fly back with me. You can meet Christopher and we can try to work this out."

I took a long look at her. For that kind of love, it was worth it. It was worth another try, another chance for her to love me.

Two weeks after we arrived back in Colorado, she left again. Her parents told her that if she took me back, they would go to court to win custody of her son. It scared her off. She told me that she was too weak. She told me she couldn't bear to lose Christopher and that he was her life now. They didn't want a drunken ex-con around their grandson.

I understood that. So, I made it easy for everyone and I left for good early the next morning.

Leaving my second wife was easier than leaving my first wife. The first time, I thought that we could make it work. I thought that I could sober up, at least, enough to be a sort of father-figure. After all, my father had done it for me and my siblings. For all the grief I gave him, he did keep us all alive, clothed, and fed. I, on the other hand, could barely do that for myself. And by the time my second wife left me for the second time, I knew that it wasn't because I wasn't trying, but rather because even if I tried every single day for the rest of my life, I would never be the man any woman deserved.

Before I rode out of town, I grabbed another bottle and drank it all before the train even reached full speed.

# *11*

AFTER MY SECOND DIVORCE, things went from bad to worse.

The doctors had lied. They hadn't really fixed my esophagus. Or if they had, they had done a bad job and I had already worn it out again. I was vomiting blood almost every day. I wasn't stupid. Deep down, I knew the end was coming, so I did what I always did when I needed help—I called Arty.

"Hello?" It wasn't Arty. It was his wife. This was going to be fun. "Hello! How are you doing today, Jane? It's Floyd."

"Of course, it is," she said. "I'm well, and yourself?"

"Well, since you asked, I'm not feeling very well at all. I was wondering if I could talk to Arty."

"He's very busy, Floyd. Now might not be the right time."

"I'm just not sure when I'll get the money to make another call like this."

She laughed. "You called collect."

"Please?" A pause. "Jane?" No answer.

"Hello? Floyd?" It was Arty.

"Hey Arty, how are ya?"

"Fine, Floyd, just tell me what you need. I already told you the bank's closed; I won't give you any more money."

"That's not why I'm calling, Art. Listen, the docs don't think I'm going to make it very long, so I just need two things from you, a ticket back to Pennsylvania and a promise."

"What's the promise?"

"That when I die you won't let them do to me what they do to all the other hobos."

"And what's that?"

"Put me in a cardboard coffin and dump me in some mass grave."

"Really? With the life that you have, your biggest worry is not having a proper funeral?"

"Come on, Arty," I said. "Can you help me or not? I can't relax until I know I'm going to be okay. Please."

Arty sighed a long sigh. "If that's all you need, then I can definitely do that for you. Just write down my number and keep it on you at all times, okay? I can't help you if I never hear if you're dead or alive."

"Thank you! Thank you, Arty. You don't know what this means."

"Yeah, yeah. As for the ticket, I can't help you with that one. I'm sure you'll find some way back."

A dial tone interrupted the conversation. I looked at the receiver. "Well, goodbye and love you too, brother." I hung up the phone and headed out to catch the next train east.

I spent a little bit of time in Harrisburg before moving west to Pittsburgh. The last time that I'd been in the hospital, the doctors had only given me a few weeks to live, but I lived in Pittsburgh for over two years.

Pittsburgh was a good city because there were a lot of corners to hustle on. I could make enough to buy four bottles in a day if I was really trying. And at night, you could hear the announcers at the sports stadiums cheering on the Pittsburgh teams as you fell asleep. In the summer, the breeze coming off the three rivers was refreshing, but in the winter, you had to get in line early to get a spot in the shelter. I didn't hang out there very often because they wouldn't let you bring booze in, but there were some nights I knew that I had to get inside just to survive.

Holidays were the worst, if I even remembered what day it was. It was one of the few days of the year where I felt as alone as I knew I was. Christmas wasn't great growing up, but at least Dad would try to make a nice meal and we would all get something we really needed. Occasionally, someone would get a really great toy and we would spend the next six months arguing over who got to play with it that day.

I knew Arty celebrated Christmas. He had kids. Maybe even grandkids by now. And my brothers and sisters—the ones who were still alive—all had kids. Somehow, they had all managed not to screw their lives up as badly as I had mine.

They say that where you grow up matters, but then how is it that Arty and I grew up in the same place, but he was at home, in front of a fire celebrating Christmas, and I was under a bridge just trying to stay warm enough to survive until New Years? Maybe it wasn't all my father's fault. Maybe having a bad mother didn't do this to me. Maybe I just wasn't cut out for normal life.

One particularly bad winter, I headed south to Washington,

Pennsylvania and lived in the woods there. They had a good mission and I was able to make some good money hustling until I passed out on Main Street one day and ended up in Washington Hospital.

My eyelids were heavy. I heard people around me. The chatter of working people, their intense, business-first voices cutting through the thick air. There were a lot of lights. It was the kind of light that you notice even with your eyes closed.

"He needs how many surgeries?"

This voice was closer. Female. Cute.

"At least three, and there's no guarantee any of them would even work."

An older man. Frustrated. Very close to me. I wanted to open my eyes, but the best I could do was scrunch my nose a little.

"I mean you've seen his chart. His lung is toast. He has a tumor on his bladder." The man was still talking. "No family, no one to call." He was talking about me. I'd heard it all before. Surgery is the only option, but first you have to get sober, get stronger. Yeah, right.

But he was wrong about the family, at least sort of.

"When he finally wakes up, we'll tell him and figure out what to do."

I didn't rush to open my eyes anymore. No reason to wake up just to hear bad news, especially if I had to hear it sober.

"You're sure there's no one we can call?" The lady's voice really was sweet.

"You can call social services and see if they have anything, but the way he looks, he's given up on asking anyone for help."

# 12

I WAS FULLY AWAKE NOW. The lights were bright, way too bright. That was always one of the worst things about being in the hospital, the other knowing how mad they would be when they realized they weren't going to get a penny out of me.

"Hello, Mr. Ridley."

"Call me Renegade."

"I'd rather not." The doctor looked down at his notes. "I could go over the list of things wrong with you right now, but I have a feeling that it won't make any difference to you."

I shrugged. "You can try."

"Well, there's a large growth on your bladder, damage to your lungs, your liver doesn't have much function..." he looked up briefly. "Shall I go on?"

"You're the boss, doc. It's up to you."

"Mr. Ridley, I'm afraid you don't see how serious this is."

"Die now, die later. We all die, doc." I could tell he was uncomfortable with my ambivalence. "The question is, do I have to die here, or can you let me go out and live the rest of my life?"

"I'm afraid there's not much left to life, Mr. Ridley. Now, I have spoken to a social worker, and we've found a spot for you at a nursing home."

"I can't afford no nursing home."

"It would be provided totally free, for the duration of your life."

Despite the fact that I knew that none of this was in his notes, the doctor kept looking down at his notes rather than into my eyes. He was young. He probably didn't know what it was like to not care if you lived or died. He probably didn't know what it was like to know that your existence or failure to exist wouldn't affect anyone or anything. Everyone would keep living their lives. Some of them even with a sense of relief.

"Still, I don't wanna be stuck inside all day."

"Well, you would be free to leave, as long as you were able."

I thought to myself. The doctor must have seen my apprehension. That, or he just really wanted to get me out of his hospital.

"It's just a bed, Mr. Ridley, a place to sleep, a place to be kept comfortable, get treatment."

I thought a bit longer, partially because I didn't know what to do and partially because I wanted to make him squirm. "Okay," I finally said. After all, what would keep me there if I decided I wanted to ditch them and hop on another train?

"Great. The social worker will be by to go over everything with you shortly. It was good to meet you, Mr. Ridley. Best of luck."

You too, young doctor. You too.

The nursing home was not bad at all. In fact, it was just like living rent-free in an apartment where people cook for you, clean for you, and check in on you every once in a while. I settled into my own sort of routine where I would wake up, have breakfast, then head down to the bar. I was the first person there in the morning.

The lady running the bar was nice and she would let me clean the bathrooms and sweep the dining area in exchange for some drinks once she opened.

Every night, I would return late and loud, drunk as a skunk. The orderlies were never too happy to see me, but I didn't care. After all, I was just waiting to die. One morning, I decided to sleep in, and I overheard the orderly complaining to the doctor.

"Well, does he cause any trouble?" the doctor asked.

"No, he's mostly just loud and drunk," she responded.

"Then just leave him be. He's got weeks to live at best and then you'll be rid of him."

Weeks turned into months. For some reason, I just couldn't seem to die until one morning when I was trying to leave for the bar.

"Is he dead?"

"He'd be better off if he was."

"Knock it off and look for a pulse."

The voices around me were muddy. I could barely hear them. *Get off! Let me sleep!* I said. No wait. I didn't say it. My mouth was dry. I tried to open my eyes, but when I did, everything was just as dark as before.

"Mr. Ridley, are you okay?"

"Call an ambulance!"

"Is there a doctor on call?"

My head hurt, but that was normal. The voices jumped over top of each other. I wanted to reach out and stop them. I wanted to tell them that everything would be fine, and ask somebody to please help me find my bourbon, but my body wasn't obeying my mind. A warm hand grabbed my wrist.

"There's a pulse. Did somebody call that ambulance?"

How many voices were there? Two? Three? Ten? Did it even matter?

None of them would be there when I woke up anyways. They rarely were. I was used to falling asleep to the sound of yelling voices and waking up in silence.

Now someone was moaning. *Dear God. Can't people even leave a man to die in peace?* Then I realized it was me. An unworldly, guttural noise. Maybe it was pain, maybe it was just to get them away. I tried to stop, but I kept moaning and moaning until all the sounds faded out to nothing, and I drifted into a warm sleep.

# *13*

I WAS AWAKE. I was usually awake more than the doctors thought I was.

They sure wandered around a lot. I took in a labored breath. I just had to pass out in the nursing home, didn't I? Now I'd have to die in a hospital instead of in my nice nursing home bed.

"Excuse me, nurse," the doctor said. "We need to arrange for this man to go to Allegheny General."

"I'm sorry, I'm not sure I'm able to do that without his doctor's approval," the nurse replied.

"Then get me his doctors," he said. "Sir—"

"What's the problem here?" Ah, a familiar voice. Not sure who, but probably one of the docs.

"This man needs to go to Allegheny General."

"With all due respect, doctor, this is the Renegade."

"I don't care who he is. This man needs treatment he can only get at Allegheny General."

"He's a homeless alcoholic. He can't even pay us!"

"Read my lips." The man's tone was intense. He was fighting. He was fighting *for me.* "Take him to Allegheny General."

No one said anything else. At least not that I heard. There were some rushed footsteps and whispered conversations, but nothing was concrete.

The next thing I knew my bed was moving. "On my count. One, two, tree."

I felt my body being lifted up and put onto a smaller bed.

This time, it was really the end. This time it was for real.

Most doctors had sounded sad when they said the words. "You're going to die." Not sad like your mother would be if she had to tell you, more like strong, like if your father had to tell you bad news.

But this doctor wouldn't even tell me to my face. Maybe he thought I was too far gone to even hear him. Maybe knowing that I had done it to myself made him sick and he couldn't stand the sight of me. Who knows?

This doctor told it to two men who would sit in my room for a few hours every day. The two men were from Alcoholics Anonymous.

"You know this man's family?" asked the doctor.

"No sir, we barely know him," the taller man said. "We just think he ought to have someone by his side through all this, don't you think?"

"Well, whether someone is here or isn't here, he's not going to need someone soon."

"What do you mean?" asked the shorter men.

"We may have done the last surgery a little too early. He

looked like he was strong enough, but his organs are failing, his vitals are fading—"

"How long do you give him, doc?" Silence.

"A few hours, at most. He probably won't be here in the morning." More silence.

The doctor didn't sound sad at all. He didn't sound like he was trying to be tough. He sounded like a judge reading off a sentence. Like a teacher delivering a lesson plan. I could tell. In his mind, it was all just a fact. He had known the whole time that he had agreed to take on my case. Part of me wondered if he would show joy or even just a little happiness if I ended up surviving this all, but I guess this was the end. I would never know.

"So what do we do? How can we help?"

The tall man was talking again, good man, he always seemed to find something to say.

"You can stay and wait if you want. Or you can go get some sleep and come back in the morning to start the burial preparations."

"Should we try to see if he has family?

I wanted to tell them to just call Arty. He'd promised he'd take care of it, but as I tried to take a breath, a deep pain gripped my chest, and I was too tired to push through the pain. *They'll find his card in your wallet,* I told myself. *And even if they don't, what's the point in worrying?*

"The hospital has a fund set aside for cases like this. You can try, but don't worry too much about it."

"Well, thank you, doctor."

"Thank you, son. You look like you've been up a while. Get some sleep. You'll be glad you did tomorrow." I heard the doctor's footsteps fade away.

"So, what do you think?" The short one this time.

"I guess we go home. He hasn't opened his eyes in hours."
A pause. "You okay?"

"Yeah, I just haven't known too many people who died. Not like this, anyways. Not alone."

"We've done what we can." The tall man sounded like he had given up. "From what the doc says, our job here is done. We did it. He's going home."

"Yeah, but home where?" Another pause.

"Hopefully somewhere...good."

"Hopefully," the short one said. "C'mon. Let's go."

Their footsteps trailed off as I thought about what the short one had asked.

*Where was I going?*

It was hard to say. I mean, where did *anyone* go?

Where did Mother go when she died? Where did Dad go? Into the earth, for sure, but it just didn't seem right that their bodies would die and then they would cease to exist completely.

But maybe I was being overly sentimental about death. I always had been.

I pried my eyes opened and looked at the sky one last time. I had looked at the sky so many times in my life. From under the bright lights of NYC to the dark plains of Nebraska. Now from this hospital room, I wondered where I would go. Was there a great beyond? Was there an afterlife at all?

Yes, I decided. Though I'd prefer that there not be, there probably was an afterlife, and it's probably set up the way most people say it is: Heaven or hell, good or bad. I didn't have a chance. What good had I done anyways? What good had I *been* anyways?

Sure, I had done a few half decent things, like bury my friend, and help those kittens. When I weighed those small acts of kindness against everything else I'd done…robbing, stealing, and mugging, there was no chance for me. My sins were so numerous; I was sure that if I put it all on one side of a scale, it would topple off its tray and onto the floor.

I took in a slow breath. *How many more do I have?* It was a shame that I had to die in a hospital. I'd much rather be breathing in the crisp air of the plains or the salty air of the seashore—anything but the stale, sterile air of a hospital.

I took another breath and was another step closer.

I knew the doctors were right this time. That was a first. Maybe it was his voice that made me really believe him. Maybe it was the fact that I felt the worst I'd ever felt. Or maybe it was the lack of alcohol. Without it lying to me, maybe I was finally seeing things clearly.

I closed my eyes and breathed again. Maybe that missionary lady knew what she was talking about. Maybe Wanda Kay's brother knew something I had never been able to grasp. Would it be worth it?

It couldn't hurt. What was there to lose?

I had never decided that there wasn't *any* God. In fact, I had decided quite the opposite. There was a God and he hated me. He hated me for sure.

But how could he hate a dying man? Not even the sourpuss doctors could hate a dying man, not even an alcoholic dying man. Everyone deserves some sense of dignity. Heck, even dear old Dad would probably give me some sympathy if he could see me laying here.

"Well boss," I said, my voice weak, barely a whisper. "I'm going to see you in a few minutes." I paused. "I ain't got no excuses."

I knew I didn't. How many dozens of people had tried to help me? Tried to save me from myself? Boston Billy's sister, both my wives, all the kind hospital people, my brother… A man with no family at all, maybe he's got an excuse, but I sure didn't. *D***** Floyd, say you're sorry for once in your life, and be genuine!*

"I guess what I want to say is I'm sorry."

A small bit of warmth filled my body. I felt light, so light I half-expected to leave my body and head on to the afterlife, but nothing changed. I kept breathing. *Maybe…*

"Boss, if You have that much mercy left—I know it's too late now, but if You'd spare me, I'll do whatever You tell me to do."

The warmth intensified and filled my whole body. It wasn't uncomfortable, but it was different, for sure. Later I would identify that moment as the moment God began to heal me.

# *14*

I WOKE UP.

Against every odd, against every doctor's word, I woke up the next morning, and the morning after that. Every day my body became stronger and my heart became more and more grateful for the opportunity just to live.

"Mr. Ridley, you're coming along quite nicely," said the doctor a few days later. I couldn't respond because I had so many tubes still in me, but I gave the doc the best smile I could. "We're going to take you to a regular room and continue your care there."

The room they put me in was nice enough. It was quieter, and I had fewer machines attached to me, so I liked that. The two men from AA continued to come, but once they realized I was going to be discharged soon, they stopped coming.

In a hospital room, you have a lot of time to think. Unfortunately, a lot of it is interrupted by the beeps of machines and the nurses coming and going all the time, day and night, but I had slept and thought in places noisier than this.

I spent a lot of time pondering my new-found religion. What did it mean, anyways? Was I going to go to church every Sunday? Was I going to be one of those people who walked down the street in a suit and tie and sang songs behind those giant doors?

I didn't want to be that, not at all. Sure, I liked the music, but I never wanted to be like those people.

Before they put me back in the nursing home, they had to put me in a rehab center so that I could learn how to eat and walk again. This was pretty embarrassing for a guy in his 60s, but it had been so long since I had been able to get out of a bed. I was thankful that they were even trying to help me.

Eventually, they moved me back into a nursing home, which just so happened to be right across the street from a nice Baptist church. My room was positioned by the front of the house, so every Sunday I heard every word of every song. I was mesmerized by the way the music seemed to flow effortlessly out of the instruments and how dozens of joyful voices all sang passionately together. They knew God; they trusted God, and so they sang to God.

I was in the nursing home so I could learn how to walk again. Something I should have mastered at age two had become a 60-year-old's nightmare. I knew, however, that if I could just get strong enough, I would be able to go inside that building and join the chorus just across the street.

Then the day came. I walked into the church one Sunday and sat in the back pew, just hoping to enjoy the music and hear the preaching more clearly.

"Hello there," a man said. I turned around and was greeted by a tall, bearded man in a grey suit. "First time? My name's John."

"Floyd," I replied, reaching out to shake his hand.

"Why don't you follow me? There are plenty of seats closer to the front," he said.

"Oh no, I'm just visiting. I'm just checking things out," I said. "Thank you."

The man nodded. "Well, I'm going to be seated in a few minutes, and there's always room next to me if you want to join me."

I thanked him and turned back to the front of the church. The tall ceilings looked majestic. I hadn't seen the inside of a church before, unless you counted the house I'd grown up in. A minute later another man invited me to sit with him, and a few minutes later, so did a whole family. Finally, I accepted and sat a few rows from the front and listened to the music and to the pastor as he preached.

After the message, the family introduced me to the pastor, who invited me to the men's group at the church. I had never really known a group of men who weren't criminals, so I accepted.

The men I met at that church helped me learn to do the things I should have learned to do as a teenager. They taught me to drive, really drive, so I would be able to pass the test and do it legally. They taught me how to open a bank account and put a certain amount into savings, and even how to get a job.

They told me I was worth something. They told me that when they looked at me, they didn't see an alcoholic or a hobo, they just saw Floyd, chosen and loved by God. Easy enough for them to say. They hadn't known me before.

One day, I was talking to my mentor, and I was telling him just how I felt.

"I know you keep telling me that God loves me…" I said.

"But what?" he asked, pouring a second cup of coffee and passing it to me.

"But I've done some pretty sorry stuff. I mean, I don't even think *I* love me."

"Well, it's a good thing God doesn't think the way we do, isn't it?" he said with a chuckle. "Floyd, there's nothing you could do that would change how much God loves you. He's loved you since the very beginning and He'll love you until the very end."

"I find that hard to believe," I said, recalling the nights I spent struggling to sleep because of the welts on my body and the days spent trying to keep my siblings alive.

He poured some sugar into his cup and stirred as he thought. "I can't explain the past, Floyd. I could try, but I'm sure I'd get a lot of it wrong. But I can explain what I know about God. And even when things looked their worst, God didn't give up on you."

"I guess so," I said.

"Everything He thinks about you is in the Bible, did you know that? Everything about how valuable you are, how precious you are, how He made you in His image, how He has a plan for you."

"Even now?"

"Especially now. People need to hear your story, Floyd. They need to know what God wants to do for them too if they just do what you did and obey Him."

It was hard to believe that I had really obeyed God. All I did was say some desperate prayer in a hospital room. But I guess I hadn't given up. I hadn't turned my back on Him.

That night, my mentor sent me home with a pack of post-it notes and a bunch of scriptures. I spent the night looking them up in my new Bible and writing down what they meant on the post-its and sticking them to my bathroom mirror.

"Holy. Righteous. Free.

Loved.

Purpose.

Significant.

Known."

Every morning, when I got out of the shower and started shaving, I would read over all the words out loud. I would say, "I am holy. I am righteous. I am free." And after a few weeks, I really began to believe them.

As I got stronger physically and mentally, I started walking everywhere I could. It always felt nice just to be alone in the sun, talking to whomever I came across, a lot like the days I was on the road. I guess I still had an itch for adventure. I would walk by shops and car dealerships and restaurants, and occasionally a bar.

Now, a few years ago, the answer was obvious. If I saw a bar, I went in it, no questions asked. Even if the Hells Angels themselves had been there all over again, I would have risked it just to get a bottle of booze. I would have risked anything. But I knew now was different.

*You told the Man upstairs that you were going to make Him proud. Right?*

Right.

*But He is proud! Look at how far you've come! You deserve to celebrate!*

Sometimes my good and bad thoughts sounded like they came from the same place. I stopped and took a few breaths. To my left, the door waited for my decision. My old friends waited for my decision too, they just didn't know it.

*If you do it, He'll be so upset.*

*If you don't do it, you'll be upset.*

And then a third voice.

*I love you Floyd, I want the best for you. Is going in that bar the best for you?*

Was it? I knew the answer was no. I knew I had made a promise to God back in that hospital room, but now? Now it was a new ball game. I wasn't fighting for my life, I was fighting for my future. When you're fighting for your life, the answer is obvious. It's simple. Live. Just live. Just do anything possible, take any avenue you need to. Just live. But when you're looking at your future, you don't know what good your decision will do, at least not in the moment.

This was a choice between obedience and disobedience. Between following what I had turned to and turning to what I had followed my whole life.

Blessings and curses. Life and death. Future and past.

My mentor had been telling me it was all about obedience and I knew that third voice was right. *It's not My best for you.* So, I started walking. First one step, heart racing. A second step. A third, now it's easier, and the next thing I knew, I was blocks away.

Up until this point, I had almost felt like I was faking it. Like I had stumbled into recovery and didn't know how to find the off ramp. A part of me figured it was possible that I would go back to drinking, probably as powerless as I had been when I stopped drinking. I figured eventually my body would realize how long it had been since it had been fueled by vodka and wine and once again, I would need a bottle like I needed air. But it never happened.

The moment I stepped past that store, everything was over. I wasn't on some path toward healing. *I was healed.* The next day when I walked by the store again, I didn't even hesitate. I had no interest. For the first time in my entire life, I wasn't remotely interested in buying a bottle. It was freedom.

I can't fully explain what happened, but I think it was the obedience. I know that if I had given in, I would never be where I am today. And it's only because I kept walking that I was able to say with confidence that I defeated my demons and I was free.

A few weeks later the doctor gave me a clean bill of health and told me I didn't have to live at the nursing home anymore. The guys from church helped me find a little one-room apartment and gave me the furniture I needed to get started. A couch, a kitchen table, a bed, and a dresser. I had my own place for the first time in decades.

I was doing a lot of odd jobs, painting, fixing things, stuff like that, when a lady approached me who worked at Greenbrier, a recovery center nearby.

"I heard your testimony, Floyd," she said, "and I think you'd make an amazing counselor."

I held back a laugh. "Me? I'm sorry, but I don't have anything more than a GED. I'd love to help if I could," I said.

"We can get you training, Floyd. I just need to know if you're interested."

I prayed about it for a while, since I had determined that I would only do what God asked me to do. The next month, I started counseling the recovering addicts down at the Greenbrier home.

It was hard. Some days it was like looking at myself in the mirror. Other days it was like looking at the people I knew on the streets. They were loud. They were combative. I shouldn't say *they* were. It was their demons that were loud. They knew they were on their way out and they hated talking to me.

"You don't get it, Floyd," they'd say to me. "It's too hard to stay sober."

"Oh really?" I replied. "I spent forty years doing what you're doing right now and it didn't get me anywhere. That is forty years of sleeping and shivering outside under a bridge while other people were inside their warm houses having meals with people who cared about them."

"But it was easy for you—"

"I had to get clean on my deathbed, and if you don't straighten up soon, that's where you're going to find yourself."

They stared at me with defeat in their eyes, shoulders hunched over. "You can't play the blame game," I said. "You are the one who can make a choice right now to do the brave thing, the hard thing, and try." They nodded at me.

"Are you ready to do that?" I asked.

Every response was different. Some men cried. Some got up and left the room. Some turned cold and refused to talk to me until days later. A few listened and did exactly what I asked them to do. *Try.*

It certainly wasn't easy to work at Greenbrier, but I liked the work. I liked feeling as though I was doing something. I was helping, at least, one of those guys get his life right before he ended up dead. So many men that I had known ended up, which is what almost happened to me.

# *15*

WHILE I WAS WORKING at Greenbrier, I got invited to speak at an Alcoholics Anonymous meeting. I had attended an AA group for a while and someone had gotten wind of my story and asked me to speak.

I almost said no, but when I prayed about it, I knew the Lord was telling me to say, "yes."

"Lord, I don't know what to say," I told Him. "I didn't even go to college. I don't know anything special."

I tried to write down a few points, but nothing happened. I crumpled up another paper and threw it into the trash can.

Talking usually came easy. Whether it was smooth-talking a businessman into buying me a drink or shooting the breeze at a hobo camp, I was never at a loss for words. Maybe it was because I was writing. I should have known better than to try to write it down. How long had it been since I'd written anything anyways? Years, probably. Maybe when I studied for the GED. Decades, and now I thought I was going to be some expert speech writer? Please.

I took a deep breath and looked around my kitchen. A few dirty dishes sat soaking in a bath of bubbles. Next to them, a hand-me-down microwave flashed the incorrect time. But... they were all mine. Dirty or broken, they belonged to me.

That was something to be proud of, I thought to myself, and I got up to finish washing the dishes. I never thought I'd own my own dishes or my own microwave at all. Heck, just three years ago, I was living under a bridge. I didn't even have enough dignity to think that it would be nice to have a microwave, let alone a whole apartment to myself.

I started to scrub the dishes, picking off the dried, leftover bits of food. Three years ago, it would have been strange to use a plate that had to be washed or to know that I would have to wash it. They didn't make you do the dishes at the homeless shelter unless you lived there permanently.

*Look how far you've come.* I felt a soft voice speak to me. I set my jaw against the onslaught of emotion.

"Only because You gave me life," I prayed out loud. It had been God, after all.

Look at me. Over sixty years old and I never had a bit of a desire to live a normal life. It hardly ever crossed my mind that there really could be a God who cared about me, but somehow, here I was.

Everything I was seemed so far away, but it still felt real. It was like I was a different person living a different life. By luck, I felt like I had been dropped into a second chance.

Somehow, I had a home, a job, a car, and friends. Somehow,

I didn't need alcohol anymore. Somehow, I didn't live for myself anymore. I couldn't possibly take all the credit.

"All I've done is obey You," I said. "And all I'll do is continue to obey You." It was my prayer every day. My prayer to stay faithful. My prayer to be the best that I possibly could be. My prayer to be used more than I ever thought was possible.

I finished the dishes and dumped the dirty water down the drain. I watched it swirl around and around until there was no trace of the dirt left. It was gone. I sat back down and put my head in my hands.

"All I want to do is please You," I said. "Give me the words to say." I sat and waited for the words, but they didn't come. In their place, however, was confidence.

I'm not who I used to be. I'm more than anyone thought I could ever become. I thought back to the post-its that I used to read every day. "I'm chosen, holy, loved, healed, and free." I know my story better than anyone. I know what God has done more than anyone. If obedience got me this far, obedience would take me forward.

A few days later, I walked into the meeting hall expecting to see a few dozen members. Usually, these things drew a bigger crowd than a normal meeting. Everyone loved to hear the speakers. It was like seeing someone who was where you wanted to be.

"Floyd Ridley?" A man in a plain button-up shirt with a clean-shaven face reached out his hand. "I'm Able; I invited you here tonight."

"Pleasure," I said, returning his handshake.

"You ready to go?"

"Just about," I said. "Is there a bathroom around here somewhere?"

"Nervous?" He chuckled. Before, I might have thought he was laughing at me, but he seemed to be good natured. "Right over there, first door to the right."

I thanked him and went to the bathroom. He was right—I was nervous—but I just needed a quiet place to pray.

"God," I prayed. "I promised I'd obey You no matter what, and You asked me to speak here. I don't know what to say, so I just ask You to give me the words that will mean something to these people and give them hope. Amen."

I looked at myself in the mirror with a clean face. Short, combed hair. It still took me a minute to recognize myself. "Let's do this."

When I walked into the room, it was packed with more people than I could have anticipated. I went up next to Able and he let me sit on a chair off to the side of the stage while he got ready to introduce me.

"Quiet down, everyone," he said. "I'm very excited to introduce our speaker for tonight. He's been in AA for a couple years now, and he has a story that I know you all are going to find both interesting and inspiring. So please, help me welcome Floyd." Able smiled and motioned for me to come up to the stage as the attendees clapped politely.

"Thank you," I said. "I never really thought I'd be a speaker at one of these things, so I never really gave much thought on what to say. So, here goes." The audience chuckled.

"I was born in the Pocono Mountains of Pennsylvania, one of ten kids and two very drunk parents." As I talked, I started to feel more relaxed and less in control. The words sometimes seemed to skip my head and come straight out of my mouth.

"At twelve years old, I would come home at one o'clock in the morning. The cops would come to my house and tell my dad, 'You've got to do something about that Floyd.' But all my dad said was, 'He'll grow out of it.'"

Then I moved on into my story about going to the military, then to jail, then skid row. I talked about getting sick, then getting sicker and finally ending up in the hospital.

"It was the most scared that I have ever been. Even getting shot didn't compare to hearing the words 'He won't survive the night.'"

Every once in a while, I would catch the face of a member of the crowd. They seemed to be listening intently, their faces scrunched up in concentration, their shoulders hunched forward as they leaned in. Able sat to the side nodding along as I spoke.

"I don't know why God saved me," I said. "But I knew that it meant I had to change the way I was living. And I knew that it wasn't enough to just try to stop drinking. I had to really stop."

I paused, waiting for the next words to come.

"I told God that I would obey Him, and that's the promise I've kept every day since then. Even when the devil tries to say to me, 'Who do you think you are?' I tell him that I'm covered by the blood."

"'What about that man you shot in Tennessee?' Covered by the blood. 'The men you mugged in New York?' Covered by the blood. 'The way you treated your family.'" I paused. "Ouch, right? But it's still covered by the blood. And it wasn't until I realized that who I was didn't matter because it didn't exist anymore that I was even able to stand before you today."

"If you let your mistakes define you, you will never move forward. But if you leave your past behind and look only toward the future, then God's gonna do something amazing with your life, if you let Him."

A few people started applauding, but they stopped as they

realized I wasn't done yet.

"If you don't mind, I'd like to close with something, I wrote."

"Last night I dreamed I passed away,
And left this world behind.
I started down that lonely road,
My destiny to find.

I came to the crossroads
Where a bright light did tell,
Turn left to Heaven my friend,
Or go right to hell.

I didn't have to study long,
I knew the path to take,
So I started down that beaten road,
That leads to Satan's place.

Satan met me at the gate,
"What's your name my friend?"
I'm Just Floyd,
Who came to a sad, sad end.

Satan went through his files and said,
"You made a mistake I fear,
You're listed as an alcoholic.
We don't want you here.""

So I went back the way I came,
And that bright sign I did see,
And turned left to Heaven,
Happy as could be.

St. Peter met me at the gate,
"Come Floyd, my friend, for you will have a new birth.
You're listed as an alcoholic-
You've had your hell on Earth.

With a heart full of joy I entered in,
And what to my surprise I see,
My old buddies Bill and Cliff,
And a friend named Lee.

There was Kathy, Tanya and Loraine,
And a gal named Bell.
And I sure was happy,
I thought they went to hell.

You can learn something from my trip,
You have a place in Heaven
If you try hard not to slip.

If someone tempts you with a drink,
When you're not feeling well,
Just tell them my loved ones,
You're going to Heaven; you've already been to hell.

# *16*

OVER THE NEXT FEW YEARS, I decided to make amends and try to reconnect with members of my family. My ex-wives were out of the picture, since they had both either married or changed their names. My children, too, were probably out of the picture, but, at least, they didn't know who I was well enough to deliberately hide themselves from me. It seemed the best place to start was Arty.

"Hello?" It was Jane who answered the phone. "Jane, it's Floyd!"

"Floyd, you're still kicking, are you?"

"Better every day, Jane. I met a Man who changed my life."

From there I told Jane the story of how I had been saved and given my life to Jesus. She was excited for me and put Arty on the phone. Arty agreed to pick me up and organize a sort of family reunion back in Milford, so I bought a bus ticket and headed east a few weeks later.

Arty and Jane met me at the bus station. I wondered if they'd recognize me. I looked better than I used to, but it had still been almost forty years since we had last seen each other.

Arty drove us straight to a nice restaurant where all my living brothers and sisters were waiting to see me again. Of course, everyone had a lot of questions, and I did my best to answer them. I guess it was probably weird for them, like meeting a long-lost relative or better yet, having dinner with a ghost. The only difference was that unlike a ghost, I was alive and there to stay.

I couldn't get myself to tell them everything. Even though I knew it was all under the blood, I was still ashamed. I didn't tell them about shooting that man in Tennessee or about how I was mugging people to stay alive. They had heard enough rumors for themselves. Heck, they heard things even worse than what really happened. One brother had been told that I was in prison in Texas while another was convinced I had been killed in Tampa. By the time I arrived, they didn't know what to believe.

Having put the record straight and catching up on forty years of family news, I headed back to Canonsburg. I still visit every so often. Three years later, Arty and I were walking together, and he said, "Floyd, I think you've finally convinced me."

"Convinced you of what?" I asked.

"That you really are sober. That there's something special in your life and that you're not going to suddenly leave us all again."

I didn't know what to say, so I waited to see if he would continue.

Arty took a big breath and stopped walking. "It was hard for me to believe that a guy of your caliber could be sober. I mean,

I saw Mom and Dad drink themselves to death, our brothers…
and none of them were half as bad as you."

He paused. "But I prayed and God told me it was true."

I cocked my head and looked at him. "So you know God,
too?"

"Yep, I sure do."

*Floyd visits some of his brothers and sisters in his hometown after fully recovering. Pictured from left to right: Lynn, Floyd, Art, Gertrude, Robert, and Richy.*

One day, in the fall of 2008, the Steelers were playing on
a Sunday afternoon when my phone rang. It was my sister-in-
law Jane.

"Listen, Arty just got a call from someone who claims to be your son."

My heart seemed to skip a beat. A million thoughts flooded into my mind at once. "My son?" I said, dumbfounded.

"Yeah. Arty didn't know if we should give him your number, but he gave us his. You can call him if you want to."

"How did he find me?"

"He called Arty at the office. I guess his mom broke down and told him your name. She knew you had a brother who was a lawyer, and he said Arty was the only Ridley lawyer he could find."

I didn't have anything to say.

"Floyd, he lives in Omaha. He seems to really think you're his dad."

"Do you think I should call him?" I asked.

Jane sighed lightly. "I think it's pretty amazing that he found you. And I know how badly you've wanted to make things right with him."

"So it's worth a shot?"

"It's up to you, Floyd," she said. "Just be careful, okay?"

I told her I would be careful, wrote down the number, thanked her and hung up the phone.

*I have a son.*

The reality of it all hadn't quite set in. What if it was a scam? It would be a pretty elaborate one; I'd give them that.

I dialed the number and waited for the phone to ring. After a ring or two, someone answered.

"Hello. This is Floyd Ridley. Who is this?" I asked.

"Chris Rochelle," he said. "My God, it's really you."

"You talked to my brother Arty?"

"Yes, I did. Well, his office. I told him I was looking for you."

He paused for a moment. "This is unreal."

"If I'm your father, then who is your mother?"

"Cathy. She lived in Omaha, Nebraska. You were married just for a few months."

It was really him. A wave of relief and anxiety came over me. I was relieved that he was who he said he was; or, at least, he was a remarkably good con man. I had anxiety that he would be mad at me or would blame me for whatever trauma I put him through by not being there for him.

"What do you do for a living?" I asked.

Chris went on to tell me that he was a warehouse worker at the time, and that he was raising his son on his own because his wife was a drug addict. "I had my own struggles with drugs too," he admitted.

*I know the feeling.*

"But I've been clean for four years now." He paused. "That's why I called you. My sponsor said it might be good for me."

"Well, I know I sure am glad you called."

"Would you want to meet?"

"Meet?"

"In person. If you could fly in, maybe we could spend the week together."

I had some money saved up, so I agreed. Just a few weeks later, I was on a plane to Omaha.

I didn't know what to expect. Every minute in the plane was bringing me closer to meeting someone I never thought I'd have the chance to meet. Sure, I thought about him before. I wondered what he looked like, whether he looked more like me or his mother. I wondered if he did okay in school or if he had a family of his own—if he liked football or baseball or something different all together. And here I was, about to find out.

I knew there was always the possibility that he wouldn't like *me.* That he wouldn't accept me as his father, or even as a friend. He might blame me for his own struggles with alcohol. It was always hard to tell what ex-addicts might be feeling or thinking.

Would I even like him? After all, this wasn't some new baby, innocent and clean. I was meeting a grown man, with all kinds of baggage and a fully-developed personality. I was about to meet someone who grew up never knowing if I was dead or alive, much less having any influence in his life. What would I even say to this boy?

As the plane touched down, I prayed one more time that God would help me, that He would restore the past and make all things new like He had already done for me so many times already.

I arrived at the baggage claim and looked around. Immediately, I spotted him. *He looked just like me.* There was a man standing next to him, who I am assuming was his sponsor. When our eyes met, he immediately started moving toward me.

"Dad," he said, reaching out and hugging me and planting a kiss on my cheek.

I was nervous. His voice sounded strained.

"Dad, I hold no animosity toward you." Now I felt my chest tighten. "All I want is a relationship with my father."

Before I knew it, tears were spilling out of my eyes. Wet patches on my shoulders let me know that Chris was crying too. We stood there in the baggage claim embracing for a while, soaking in all that time and alcohol had cost us.

When we finally separated, I saw that his sponsor had been crying. So were two ladies from my flight who were standing a few feet away watching us.

"Let's get your bags," Chris said. "I want you to meet my daughter."

Chris, his sponsor, and I all piled into a car and drove to his apartment. It was a humble place, but it was plenty big enough for him and his daughter. A woman, I later learned was his girlfriend, handed Chris a baby. Chris in turn handed the baby to me.

"This is your granddaughter."

I accepted the baby and the blankets she was resting in.

"She's six months old," he said.

I looked down at her face, soft and round. Her eyes were peacefully closed as she rested and her little rose lips occasionally moved in a sucking motion. She was the picture of innocence and perfection, and she was finally restored to me.

I looked upward. "What happened here?" I said to no one in particular. "How did this happen to me?"

Chris's sponsor took a step toward me. "You know what happened, Floyd." He rested a hand on my shoulder. "You didn't pick up a drink these last four years, and God honors that."

It still seemed too good to be true. I was amazed that God had found me worth saving and healing my body, but to have a car, and an apartment and a job…and now a son and a granddaughter! It was more than I ever could have possibly deserved. I guess that's why they call it grace.

We visited with each other for a little while and then caught a few hours of rest. The next day, Chris took me to a recovery meeting to speak. "This is my dad," he said. "We didn't know each other for the longest time, but I want you all to hear his story."

It was amazing to be called Dad. Sometimes it's easier to say that you've forgiven someone than to actually do it, but Chris seemed to have written off the past as just that—the past.

From there, a lot of healing took place and we agreed

that we would write and keep in touch. The next summer, he came and visited me and spoke with me at a recovery meeting. Sometimes, alcoholics can see things from only their own perspectives, but there's a lot of pain and confusion that goes on that you never see.

Chris told the audience what it was like to grow up without a dad and to only know me through the stories that his mother told him. "'He's a drunk. He rides the trains. He's no good and he'll never amount to anything,' she said to me. And I heard that any time I asked about my dad and even when I didn't ask," Chris said.

"Even when I told her that I had met Dad and that he was clean and sober and doing great, she laughed at me, and said, 'It won't last.'"

It was hard to hear that Cathy still had those kinds of feelings toward me, but at the same time, she had not had the chance to get to know me now, sober and living for the Lord.

My son and I still talked, wrote and sent pictures. He had another child—a son—and he's going to get married to the boy's mother. I told him that he has a sister, and I promised him that if I ever found her, I'd let him know.

I had tried finding Jennifer before, but her mother had remarried and changed both Jennifer's last name and her own. I understood that she probably didn't want to be associated with me, but it made trying to make things right hard.

Finally, one of my friends had the idea to look up Wanda's maiden name on the Internet. Sure enough, we found her mother's obituary and Wanda and her daughter Jennifer were listed as surviving family members, Wanda and Jennifer Long.

We did some extra searching and found out that my ex-wife now lived in Ogallala, Nebraska where she was a counselor for married couples—believe it or not.

I called her office. They wouldn't let me speak to her, but they let me leave a message.

"My name is Floyd Ridley," I said. "And I would like to ask Wanda Kay if she would please give my number to Jennifer Nicole."

That's all I did. That's all I could do. If she didn't want Jennifer to meet me, I knew I was going to have to be okay with that. So, I left it alone.

A few months later, I was watching the Steelers play again when my phone rang. I didn't recognize the number, but I didn't think anything of it. My number gets passed around to so many alcoholics and bums who need help. "Hello?"

"Hi." The female voice on the other end hesitated. "Is this Floyd Ridley?"

"Yes, it is."

"Hi." Again, another hesitation. "This is Jennifer Nicole."

Now I was the one who hesitated. I was stunned.

"You don't have to say anything," she said. "I just found out you were alive. Mom finally gave me your phone number. I've had it for a while, but I didn't call because I didn't even know if I wanted to. I guess I've just heard so many negative things about you that I didn't know if I wanted to rekindle things or not."

"I'm really glad you called."

"Me too," she said. "I guess I just want to get to know you, or at least try."

"Do you want me to come out and meet you?" I asked.

"No, no," she said. "I don't think that's a good idea right now. I can't handle that. I'm still trying to wrap my mind around the fact that you're alive. Mom always told me you were dead somewhere. Talking to you right now is like talking to Lazarus."

"Okay," I said.

I must have sounded disappointed because she quickly added, "I'm not saying never. I just need you to give me some time to get my head around this, you know, the fact that you're alive. But, we could write and send each other pictures if you want to do that."

I agreed, happy for any way to get to know my daughter.

We exchanged addresses and for the next two years we wrote. I sent her pictures of me and she sent me pictures of herself and her family. And every Sunday night, I would call her and we would talk on the phone for a few minutes.

I didn't push the issue of visiting because I was just so thrilled that she wanted to get to know me at all. I sent her pictures of my apartment and my church. I told her about her brother, which made her really happy. She hadn't known she had a half-brother. She told me about her work and about how she and her husband had met.

Finally, one night she called me and said, "Floyd,"—she couldn't call me "Dad" because really I wasn't her dad in her eyes since another man had raised her—"I think it's time we met."

We worked out a plan where she and her family could meet both Christopher and me. It turned out that she only lived a seven-hour drive from Omaha, so she agreed to drive up if I could fly to Omaha. When I told Chris the plan, he was excited to get to meet his sister, so he agreed, and we set the date.

Chris dropped me off at my hotel and I felt like I was about to meet him all over again. The same thoughts flooded my mind. Her kids were older, much older than Chris's daughter had been. And she was married, so there was another person I had to meet.

Would she like me? Sure, things had gone well over the phone and through our letters, but what about in person? How would her kids react to seeing me for the first time?

The next day Chris, his fiancée, and I all climbed in to their car and drove to Red Robin, where we had agreed to meet Jennifer and her family for dinner. It was like a movie—we both pulled into the parking lot at the same time and parked right next to each other.

Full of nervous excitement, I got out of the car and waited.

Jennifer let both of her little girls come out of the car. They were five and six years old at the time. They looked up at me and ran toward me yelling, "Grandpa, Grandpa!"

Each one grabbed a leg and I felt myself beginning to weep. Still with the girls on each leg, Jennifer came up wrapped her arms around me, kissed my cheek, and said into my ear, "Forty years is too long."

We stood in the parking lot hugging for a few moments before we separated and made introductions. She and Christopher hit it off right away. It was like a dream.

The next day, we decided to meet at the zoo where the grandkids led me around from exhibit to exhibit, excitedly yelling, "Look at this, Grandpa!" and "Over here, Grandpa!"

That night, we went to the hotel and talked in the lobby for hours. I finally got to tell her about my life, who I was and how I got sober and found the Lord. I told her about how I was Christian now and I was working with other addicts as a counselor, trying to help them find the same freedom that I had found. I couldn't tell her everything; I couldn't bring myself to because I still felt a lot of shame about what I had done. But she nodded and listened politely the whole time.

"I know you've done a lot of things, but I'm so glad you're here now," she said. "Not everyone gets that kind of a second chance."

The next day, we went swimming in an indoor swimming

park and it was like we had known each other for years.

The next morning, I went to their hotel to say goodbye. As we packed up their SUV, Jennifer's two daughters grabbed me by the legs again. "Grandpa's coming with us, right?" they asked.

"Not now," I told them. They protested, but I told them that I would do my best to see them as soon as I could. Truthfully, I didn't know if I would get to see them again. I wanted to honor Jennifer's wishes and while a lot of good had come from the trip, I wasn't sure what she would want to do next.

Once the girls were buckled in the car, I gave Jennifer a hug and thanked her for the visit. "I hope some healing can take place in our relationship." She smiled at me and thanked me for coming too.

Watching them drive away, I started weeping. She had to process this visit too, and maybe she didn't even really want to connect with this stranger who was supposed to be her father. But I knew for me, the visit had only strengthened the love I felt for her and her family. I didn't want to let them go.

I took a breath and directed my thoughts toward Heaven in a prayer.

A few days later, my daughter called me.

"Dad," she said. My heart jumped. "I had a lot of time to think about things. You're my father. We're the same blood and I really feel like I need to—and want to—call you Dad."

"What happened?" I asked.

"I came home and I said to my husband, 'You know what happened during this visit? I think I fell in love with my father.'"

I cried like a baby. You can't buy a statement like that from your own daughter. It was a gift from God.

It's been a big transition, to go from a man with no family to a man who not only has sisters and brothers but also a son,

*Floyd is reunited with his son, daughter, and their families for the first time.*

a daughter, and grandchildren. This is all new to me, so I feel like I am walking on eggshells.

I pray a lot.

I'm thankful for my pastor, who helps me as best he can. He teaches me what he knows, and God guides me and shows me what I need to do next. I never dreamed in my wildest imagination that I would have my son and daughter back in my life. I thought that losing my family was just the cost of living over forty years as an addict, a price I would pay until I died, but God had other plans.

As I continued living my life, I found that just going to AA meetings was not enough. My faith helped, and prayer helped, but I felt like there was more that God wanted to do in my life. While I was talking to my pastor about this, he encouraged me to seek out the baptism in the Holy Spirit. So, week after week, I asked God to give me the baptism of the Holy Spirit, the power to help me to stay clean and sober and to have more power to help other people get clean too. At that time, I was ministering to people on the street every week, taking them sandwiches and hot chili and talking to them about how much God loved them and the life that He wanted for them.

But working with addicts is not easy. I had been spat at, yelled at, and mocked. It was part of the territory, but it was tiring.

I knew that I had the Holy Spirit when I got saved, but I needed more power because of the people who I was dealing with. And that power, I knew from the Bible and from my pastors, was the Holy Spirit.

One Sunday, I was praying in church during altar time, when something that felt similar to warm water pouring down my head. The intensity of the feeling caused me to kneel down on the ground, and I started speaking to God. As I spoke, I realized, it wasn't English that I was speaking, but some other language, something Heavenly. I didn't fully understand what was happening, but I didn't fight it. As I spoke, I felt strength bubbling up in me.

I felt like I came alive.

I wanted to jump up and run out and tell everyone about Jesus and what had just happened. But whatever I did, I wanted to receive the gift that I had just been given with thankfulness and show God that I would use it and not abuse it. As soon as it happened, I realized that I had the power available to me where I could stand against all odds. I had no fear of going to certain places in Pittsburgh to preach the gospel. I used to steer clear of certain areas of the city, but now the fear was gone because I knew who I was and I knew the power that was within me.

I asked my pastor why God would choose to give me the Holy Spirit and use me to reach people living on the streets when I had lived most of my life so terribly. He said simply, "The people in the pews won't do it. God will use whoever is willing."

So, every day I do whatever I can to feed that spirit. I'm so thankful for it. I need to feed it with obedience. And every time I obey God, I feel like He fills me up with strength and power for the next thing that I need to do. He's always there to fill my cup when I ask Him.

But that wasn't the end of what God had for me.

Having my family back was a miracle. God had completely restored them to me despite everything that I had done to mess up my relationship with them in the past. But even as my heart was rich in love, I was struggling with my health.

Since I had recovered, I had been put on the waiting list for a lung transplant. In fact, I had to quit my job at Greenbrier because the work that I was doing was too hard on my heart.

Still on the transplant list, in June of 2018, I went to my doctor for a checkup. After some routine scans to check on the health of my remaining lung, the doctor called me into his office.

"How are you feeling, Floyd?" he asked.

I took a deep breath in through my nose, just to show off how good I felt. "Feeling fine, doc."

"That's good to hear," he said, adjusting his glasses and tapping on his computer. "I wanted to ask you where you thought I should put the new lung when we get it."

"Well," I said, "I guess you could just put it right where the one they took out used to be."

"What lung are you talking about, Floyd? What I'm looking at here on this scan are two perfect lungs."

My eyes must have widened to the size of dinner plates. *Two* lungs?

"You're sure?" I asked.

"I'm looking at the scan right now, and there are two good lungs. There's no evidence that you ever had a lung taken out."

After that, the doctor made some calls and found the doctor who had taken out my lung.

"I remember you, Floyd," he said. "I remember we thought we'd killed you by taking out your lung too early, before you were stronger."

"So, what do you make of this?" I asked.

The doctor sighed and shook his head. "Some things happen that I just can't understand, and you know what I do with them? I file them in my miracle box."

Looking back, I realized that I had felt stronger and less short of breath in the previous days. A few weeks before then, Evangelist Jonathan Shuttlesworth had prayed for God to increase the anointing on my life and just a few days before I went to the doctor, my pastor had prayed for God to give me "total restoration."

And that's exactly what He did.

Now, I don't need to use oxygen at night anymore. In fact, I go down to the track and run laps just to show off.

I've come a long way in the last decade. Even when I was on the streets, I knew I didn't want to die a drunk junkie, homeless in the gutter. What a terrible epitaph! I never dreamed I would be doing everything that I am now, helping people who are homeless and struggling, spending holidays with my family, and traveling around telling my story. Now, I can almost hear God saying, "You started out fast and loose, but you ended up okay. Come on in; I have a reward for you."